I0820888

AN OPEN HEART
THE KEY TO SELF-LOVE

AN OPEN HEART
THE KEY TO SELF-LOVE

CLAUDIA FARIA CARVALHO
PHOTOGRAPHS BY CLAUDIA FARIA CARVALHO

POINTED LEAF PRESS

CONTENTS

Preface 13
Whispers of Love 15
PART I: BEGINNINGS 16
In the Garden of My Mind 19
Sacred Footsteps 42
Spiritual Riches in Varanasi 42
The Divinity of Nature 48
The Sacredness of Banyan Trees 51
Bali's Rich Spiritual Traditions 52
The Interconnectedness of East and West 52
PART II: THE TAPESTRY OF MY LIFE 60
Unveiling My Inner Child 63
Following My Bliss 70
The Seed of Consciousness 76
PART III: VISIONS ALONG THE PATH 84
An Open Heart 87
Reconnecting with My True Nature 91
The Gift of Life 96
Forging Paths 99
The Union of Opposites 100
The True Meaning of Religion 104
The Message of a Dahlia 108
Navigating the Depths of My Soul 108
The Seven Faces of the Soul 111
Journeying Through Fairy Tales for Personal Growth 114
A Journey to Liberation 126
Whispers of Eternity 131
The Forbidden Fruit 135
PART IV: INTEGRATING CONSCIOUSNESS AND PHYSIOLOGY 138
The Science of Life and Healing 141
Meditating, Transcending, Uniting 143
PART V: FINDING RESOLUTION 150
Celebrating My Reunified Self 153
Acknowledgments and About the Author 158
Bibliography and Recommended Reading 159
Index 160

PREFACE

In the tranquil depths of my inner world, where thoughts gently dissolve and the heart's voice speaks more clearly than words, I have discovered a sanctuary of wisdom.

This memoir captures moments of quiet soulful introspection, where symbols and metaphors emerge from the depths of my being, from my subconscious and superconscious mind. These expressions provide insights into profound past memories and timeless truths that resonate with my innermost self.

The seeds for this book were planted decades ago during my peaceful meditation sessions, when I first began to understand and write down my inner visions and their symbolism. Through these visions, my soul gently unveiled its secrets. I gained insights filled with deep significance that required understanding through my heart to uncover their deepest and fullest meaning. I use these revelations as a tool for my personal growth. Through the disciplined practice of recording my visions and insights, I have crafted a patchwork of spiritual awareness that maps out my journey and purpose.

What unfolds within these pages is more than just a collection of personal reflections—it is a journey back to the essence of who I am, propelled by a ceaseless quest to understand the nature of love. This journey illuminates the profound truth that finding oneself often requires the courage to first lose oneself in the pursuit of love and truth.

WHISPERS OF LOVE

Deep within me resides a gentle, loving, nurturing presence.
It is my higher self, a spark of consciousness, the experience of unbounded love, my true nature.
Consciousness wants to know itself.
It speaks with the voice of remembrance.
Gentle whispers of love illuminate my path, guiding me beyond the veils of ignorance to greater understanding and harmony.
My dearest one, you are the love, my heart's beating song.
You embody bliss, joy, innocence, and laughter.
You anchor me; you are my authentic self.
You are my vision, the touchstone of my character.
You, my inner light, have awakened my spiritual nature,
and for that I am eternally grateful.

PART I
BEGINNINGS

IN THE GARDEN OF MY MIND

In the vast expanse of my inner world I roam freely, exploring its boundless depths. Like a river that never rests, my memories ebb and flow—moments of joy, laughter, sorrow, and reflection. Each memory adds a unique hue to the tapestry of my life, creating a rich collection of experiences that shape who I am.

At the heart of my journey lies the intricate interplay of relationships, which resembles a captivating kaleidoscope. Here, emotions, interactions, and shared moments intertwine, creating connection based on understanding and mutual growth.

Sometimes harmonious and effortless, other times demanding patience, compromise, and resilience, each step in this dance enriches humanity with layers of depth and meaning.

In my travels, I encounter a rich mix of cultures, traditions, philosophies, and spiritual practices. Each experience unfolds as a thread in the tapestry of my unique fabric, expanding my perspective and understanding of the world.

As I wander deeper through the garden of my mind, I gather petals strewn along the path. Each petal holds the memory of cherished moments, experiences, and lessons learned, encapsulating the essence of my being. These petals, like fragments of a mosaic, come together to form the mandala of my life's journey.

As I delve into the depths of my essence, I expand beyond the layers confined by my personality, ego, and conditioned narratives. With each exploration, I uncover the essence of my soul's purpose and the yearnings of my heart—jewels hidden beneath layers of sediment, waiting to be discovered and polished into brilliance.

In the vast expanse of my consciousness, each desire and dream shines like a distant star in the night sky, guiding me forward with its luminous presence.

Each one holds its own brilliance, illuminating the path and inspiring me to reach for the heavens.

As I wander through the threads of my past, I embroider my present with the wisdom of olden tales and the colors of my heart's desires. With each stitch I weave vibrant hues and positive choices aligned with my soul's purpose, enriching the fabric of my life.

I feel that life unfolds according to divine timing, revealing itself in a sequence beyond my control and immediate comprehension. I move and flow through my divine rhythm, always seeking wisdom over destination. With each step I cultivate patience, nurture resilience, and embrace the lessons with grace, knowing that every moment adds to the grandeur of existence's harmonious song.

I am in the second half of my life, and I find that is never too late to nurture my abilities and nourish my soul. The wisdom gained through years of experience becomes a powerful catalyst for insight and transformation, a gift of maturity that brings me clarity, purpose, and a connection to the essence of my being.

In the fertile land of my heart, a garden of magic unfolds—a sanctuary where seeds of gratitude and healing blossom into radiant blooms of hope and renewal.

I am grateful for the support and nourishment from nature and my fellow travelers on this path. It is a testament to the interconnectedness of existence. In the flames of love and passion, I rediscover my life energy.

Freeing my inner impulses allows me to authentically express my true nature. This driving force propels me beyond the chaos that may surround me. As my heart relaxes, a profound transformation unfolds, nurturing a deeper love and compassion within me.

As I embrace the quietude within, I rediscover the simplicity of my own essence, an inner sanctuary where the truest version of myself blossoms, free from the tangle of external complexities. I am releasing the life I envisioned

to embrace the life I have longed for. As I mature and develop, I discern a metamorphosis within. I gradually reveal and embrace myself, cherishing my distinct qualities, both strengths and vulnerabilities, appreciating my genuine individuality and authentic nature. This journey leads me to a deep sense of contentment, self-respect, and inner peace.

I choose to pursue what inspires me. I surround myself with people who uplift and support my growth. In love I find freedom as I merge with my heart and with all that is. As I relax, let go and surrender, I find stillness within. I feel my energy flowing.

In the realm of creativity, I uncover the essence of who I am. I draw inspiration from the beauty and splendor of nature. Its boundless array of shapes, textures, and hues are a form of creativity that surpasses all human comprehension. Nature's wisdom fuels my imagination. Photography is my love, learning my passion and creating beauty is my purpose.

Through life's twists and turns, my dharma gleams like a guiding star within, lighting my path and aligning me with my soul's purpose. It calls me to create a life that nurtures my true self, filling me with peace and fulfillment as I move in harmony with the universe. The seeds of spiritual expansion have taken root, yearning for the nourishing touch of love. Like a tender garden, my soul craves care and attention to flourish, seeking the gentle embrace of mindfulness and affection to continue its growth and blossoming.

As a determined seeker, I trace the roots of my lineage, the rich cultural, familial, and spiritual heritage, seeking enlightenment in my past. Amid the mystical woods of my memories, each tree branch becomes a storyteller, whispering echoes of my childhood, stirring emotions, and evoking forgotten tales of yesteryears.

I was born and raised in Brazil, my beautiful country, which is known for its varied landscapes and dense forests, including the famous Amazon. We are a very warm, loving, cheerful, hospitable, and friendly people. We have great respect for the family. I grew up in an environment defined by my family values and tradition. I came of age in a country of natural wonders, in a vibrant culture whose mystical approach to life resonated with my true nature.

I have a deep heart connection to Brazil, but I could not stay there forever. I needed more freedom and space to explore and express myself. I write these lines now, some thousands of miles away from my birthplace. So much has happened, there is so much to tell—50 years of blessings and setbacks, growth and stagnation, expansion and contraction. It has taken that long. I am beginning to understand and cultivate a true connection with my authentic self and identity. I embrace my journey as my truth, the beginning of a deeper reconnection with my true nature. This ongoing process is a journey of healing scars through the transformative powers of love, compassion, and understanding.

In the corridors of my memory, the image of a little girl emerges—good, nice, loving, and sometimes touched by the flame of anger. I grew up insecure and shy. I was the innocent teenager searching for fairy tales. I am the daughter, the sister, the wife, the mother, the friend. I love, observe, and learn. I have a very curious, inquisitive nature. I enjoy adventure, traveling, and meeting people from different cultures with different philosophies. I am the dreamer of inspiring and audacious dreams. I am a woman. I have loved conditionally and unconditionally.

I am also a child deeply connected to God, experiencing a profound sense of belonging and closeness that surpasses the limitations of language. This connection provides me comfort, guidance, and a deep awareness that a higher power, a divine presence, lovingly nurtures and leads me on my life's path. I am sharing my story with you, not because I have reached any lasting conclusion, but because it is my story lived and guided by my heart's desires, by my visions, dreams, and experiences. This is a story with many chapters and yet many more to come.

My soul yearns to be free and to be able to express its true nature, to explore its gifts and strengths, to be open to new possibilities. I feel like a student of life.

I totally resonate with Michael Roads' words from *Pan … and Me*: *"I am life discovering life, in a human form with no beginning or ending. Where am I going in my eternal journey? I have no idea as a human person, as an expression of divine being the question is meaningless. I am the journey which I am journeying."*

In the vast expanse of existence, I wander,
A human vessel, with no beginning nor end.
Where am I bound in this eternal quest?
As a mere mortal, such questions find no rest.
Yet, as a spark of the divine,
I am the journey itself,
Each step a sacred dance, every moment a gift.
So I journey on, not toward, nor away,
But simply being, in the eternal play.

Indeed, spending a lifetime seeking answers to these uncharted questions is how my imagination has expanded and evolved. With each inquiry I dive deeper into the realms of possibility, allowing my creativity to flourish and my understanding to deepen. It is through this exploration that I define the true magic of imagination—the ability to continually stretch the boundaries of what I know and envision the boundless potential of what I do not know.

In my seventh decade now, I feel I have something meaningful to say. Speech, as a poet once said, has now become the twin of my vision. My words and my visions mingle like lovers in my book. There is a deluge of feelings and words. In moments of turbulent emotion, words become vessels, carrying the currents of my inner world to the surface. It is within this deluge of feelings and words that I discover the raw authenticity of my human experience, where the depth of my emotions finds its voice. I experience a clarity of consciousness, an epiphany of self-awareness.

Where do I begin?

As I explore the depths of consciousness, I come to realize that the very essence of what I cannot fathom resides within me. It is a reminder that my potential for growth, discovery, and imagination knows no limits. The unexplored realms of my inner world are as infinite as the cosmos itself; I journey into the ever-expanding universe of my mind. It is within this limitless landscape that I uncover the interconnectedness between the microcosm of my inner world and the macrocosm of the universe.

I am resilient. I write to express my awe.

Indeed, we continuously uncover scientific formulas that accelerate the world's pace. We construct homes for security and stability. We experience love, hatred, remembrance, and forgetfulness. Through it all, I remain inquisitive and contemplative, always examining and questioning the nature of existence. Writing anchors me. Like life, writing stimulates me to face up to myself, everyday. In these pages I share my story because there is so much more to understand and because writing gives me answers.

Yes, the words guide me. When I write I become as unguarded and as inquisitive about life as the child I once was. And this is part of the joy, and the power, older age bestows on some of us. Fearlessness. As I get older, I feel like I am born again. I am free and curious, uninhibited and unembarrassed, innocent and eternal. Honest. I know that my story will never finish—how can it, while I am still here? My story will never conclude—how can it while I am still growing? And that is the process of writing, unpredictable and unscripted.

Life is a dynamic process of contraction and expansion. We can feel the tension of opposing forces in the ups and downs of our lives. In one moment, we demonstrate fortitude, courage, and control; in the next, we seem beaten and vulnerable, and our heart is aching. Just be patient in the process of unfolding. Courage is a sublime armor of human strength capable of conquering impatience and fear. It is the shield that guards me as I face the unknown;

it is the sword that cuts through the crisis of doubt and the beacon that lights my path in times of darkness. The threads of complexity that wove my life are inherited from those who came before me and carry the legacies of diverse qualities and unique features. Yet, when I touch my inner core, the wholeness is awe-inspiring.

The memory of my mother and father evokes a sense of subtlety and complexity—a portrait of individuals whose lives were textured by layers of depth and nuance. They were both warriors who each faced the unique challenges of a different time.

Since I was a young child, I had the gift of a heightened intuition, a quiet guidance from within, a precious aspect of my being. It is the voice of my superconscious wisdom, a guiding force that extends beyond the boundaries of logical reasoning, enabling me to sense, to understand, and to perceive the hidden depths of life and existence. I feel that by trusting my intuition I make choices aligned with my innermost truths and the world around me.

I have so many voices inside me that come from past memories, fragments, sorrows, and joy. How do I recognize where the voices are coming from? To recognize the origin of the voices within, I have to take a significant step by becoming aware of the thoughts and emotions that arise inside me. I have to discern whether my inner whispers are rooted in fear and self-interest, if they tend to judge, to criticize or to compare, or if they promote growth, understanding, and kindness.

The voice of my higher self is always compassionate. It offers clarity, insight, and a broader perspective, beyond my personal desires. My inner voice is aligned with my deepest values, leading me toward authenticity. I have named this inner voice *Ananda*—the voice that guides me toward my destiny, a steadfast source of wisdom and inspiration as I walk my unique path.

I believe in destiny and soul agreements before birth, that my life is guided by a preexisting plan or map. I believe my journey in life has a purpose, and I feel a

profound interconnectedness with the people I encounter. Each experience and lesson contributes to the expansion of my consciousness.

In a brief moment at a gathering, I locked eyes with a stranger, and within that gaze a silent prophecy unfolded—the whisper of a union meant for learning and growth. Reflecting on my marriage, I now see it as a vibrant canvas woven from myriad colors and shapes, rich with opportunities and new experiences. I was blessed with the precious gift of space and freedom, and I learned to honor my soul's needs. With a deep gratitude, I embrace my destiny and the unwavering support of the universe. Following my passions, pursuing personal goals, and nurturing my individuality have given me the courage to spread my wings and soar toward this sacred realm.

After 50 years together, guided by the stars, we made the heartfelt decision to go our separate ways. Our three sons stand as pillars of love, care, integrity, and character, the precious fruits of our shared journey. Through their laughter and tears they have bestowed upon us cherished memories and boundless affection. Now, as they embark on their own paths alongside their loving wives, our family expands joyfully with presence of darling grandchildren, each symbolizing the beauty of life's cycle. They are my favorite hellos and the hardest good-byes, imbuing our lives with immeasurable joy and meaning.

I was as much of a dreamer as most girls of my generation. I thought it entirely natural to dream of a romantic, fairy tale–like love, especially when surrounded by stories that paint such vivid pictures of perfect relationships. Immersed in the captivating tales, I found solace in the character's yearning for love—a reflection of my own longing. Embracing the interplay between romance and true love, I longed for a connection infused with both passion and tenderness.

Little did I know that my life's journey would be an odyssey. Exploring deeply within myself, through many trials and revelations, I eventually discovered the essence of love at the core of my being, a love beyond the fleeting allure of romance. My life is illuminated by a guiding spark, a tiny golden seed nestled in my heart that shines with wisdom. This seed has been a beacon bestowing insights, fostering self-reflection, and validating my cherished values. It is through this inner light that I have navigated life's path, drawing strength and wisdom and allowing it to shape my understanding of my place within the world.

In the labyrinth of my fate, I found myself at times crawling through familiar roads, feeling imprisoned in repetitive cycles dictated by ingrained conditioning that provided a sense of safety and comfort while hindering the expansion of my spirit. Recognizing my limitations, I chose to carve out space within myself for new possibilities and experiences. Embracing the discomfort of change, I liberated my spirit to soar into unexplored realms.

As time went by, clarity dawned upon me like a gentle sunrise. I came to realize that amid life's challenges, my deepest pain does not stem from external wounds, but from the ache of disconnection from my true nature, from the eternal sanctuary of self-love. I realized that nurturing an intimate connection to myself is the cornerstone of enduring happiness, peace, and fulfillment. Healing unfolds as a solitary journey, each step in its own rhythm, guided by my readiness to search further.

Paulo Coelho, a Brazilian writer, reminds us that destiny is often aligned with what we have always yearned to achieve. Delving into the depths of my soul, I am able to unearth my deepest heart's desires, revealing the essence of my innermost aspirations. When I'm in harmony with my true nature, I feel uplifted. This joy paves the way for my best life to unfold.

Thirty years ago, at the C. G. Jung Institute of New York, amid a quiet mood of contemplation and introspection, my teacher asked a question as profound as the cosmos itself: "What is your purpose in life?" Without a moment's pause, I said words that expressed a longing to reconnect with my deepest essence and find solace within myself. This declaration became a gentle murmur, a quiet sigh, a sense of delicate intimacy and tranquility.

In my quest for self-discovery, I immersed myself in the timeless wisdom of mystics. As I explored deeply, hidden truths gently unfurled like delicate petals,

expanding my consciousness and igniting a sense of remembrance. My inner visions help me to understand the symbolic messages of the universe received through my heart. Messages with subtle nuances and patterns underlie all creation, expressing the interconnectedness and interdependency of all things.

Meditation emerged as a transformative tool, a bridge spanning the realms of thought and emotion. With each breath, I journey deeper into the depth of my being, transcending the ceaseless chatter of the mind and the maze of emotions. I immerse myself in the boundless reservoir of my innermost self. The chaos of the world fades away and I experience a serene sanctuary. I bask in the tranquility and peace of my core.

Another adventure is a series of past-life regressions. As I go through the corridors of time, I uncover hidden layers of history and information. I access a library of knowledge and wisdom encoded in a nonphysical place, the Akashic Records. I see how past impressions shape my present reality. I unearth fragments of myself lost through disconnection and transcend the constraints of lifetimes, gaining a deeper understanding of my soul's healing process.

Participating in spiritual retreats guided by revered teachers and gurus such as Maharishi Mahesh Yogi, Gurumayi Chidvilasananda, Eckhart Tolle, Deepak Chopra, and Paramahansa Yogananda's disciples, I discovered solace and enlightenment. Each teacher shared their own special wisdom and practices, which deeply enriched and nourished my spiritual development. These retreats became sacred spaces where I could find guidance and inspiration.

Engaging in higher self meditation, I feel enveloped by an unbounded love. My essence shines brightly, guided by deeper wisdom and teachings from within. I experience an alignment with universal laws.

In my travels, I encounter countless radiant souls—individuals with bright hearts and enlightened minds—who illumine my path. Their presence serves as a beacon of inspiration, igniting within me the desire to deepen my understanding of existence itself.

SACRED FOOTSTEPS

> **Long is my never-ending journey.**
> **Myriads of footsteps expanding in different beats,**
> **On different continents, leaving their marks along the way!**
> **This is the burning quest for my truth,**
> **Burning as the blazing sand under my feet, as the ever-reigning sun.**
> **This is a quest filled with wonder and desire.**
> **It guides me to open seas of experience,**
> **Urging me to acknowledge a deep intimacy with my human nature.**

Driven by a deep curiosity and yearning for enlightenment, I embarked on an exploration of the world I inhabit.

My quest was not just about traversing geographical landscapes, but immersing myself in the rich tapestry of cultures, people, and the myriad facets of the universe nestled within each unique society.

With an open heart, I search for enlightening experiences. Among diverse cultures, I discover a symphony of traditions, beliefs, and customs, each contributing a verse to the universal melody of existence, enriching my understanding of the interconnectedness and beauty inherent in the world.

SPIRITUAL RICHES IN VARANASI

While traveling through India, I discovered a country with a kaleidoscope of traditions and an unparalleled spiritual richness that touched my soul. Varanasi, the city of Shiva, stands as a living testament to this culture, pulsating with an ancient heartbeat that resonates through its streets and along the sacred Ganges River. In this vibrant city, I find myself immersed in cleansing rituals, devotion, and spiritual fervor. Early in the morning I cross the Ghats, the steps along the river where fires are still glowing from last night's purification ceremony. I see a woman bowing her head, holding a handful of the supposedly cleansing water, then slowly spilling it over her body several times. It all happens in silence and

in a peaceful simplicity. That moment feels like the bliss of a certainty, where people live their lives in accordance with their beliefs and faiths. India is a land of contradictions, the meeting point of myriad religions and diverse cultures. Amid the apparent chaos, a remarkable order is noticeable, and somehow everyone coexists harmoniously. I hear the sounds of traffic, loud horns, and rattling motorbikes, and even though at first, everything seems exhaustingly chaotic, in the end, the immense commotion blends and enriches the vibrant energy of the city—its people flowing in the streets, the youngsters, beggars, tourists, people on bicycles, and motorcycles passing by, always moving, praying, talking.

Vedic philosophy, originating from the ancient culture of India as far back as 6,000 years ago, presents certain key philosophical concepts that resonate deeply within me. These concepts provide me with a spiritual framework, sense of belonging, and feeling of interconnectedness with the universe. Some of the concepts of the Vedic tradition, like karma, dharma, moksha, brahman, and atman, have deeply influenced my spiritual and ethical outlook. These timeless principles offer valuable guidance on how to navigate life with mindfulness and purpose, leading to a more fulfilling and harmonious existence.

1. **KARMA** refers to the law of cause and effect. It suggests that our actions, intentions, and deeds have consequences, and what we sow, we shall reap.

2. **DHARMA**, in its essence, speaks to the belief that each one of us has a unique purpose and role to fulfill in life. Living in alignment with one's dharma is the path to a life that is meaningful and deeply fulfilling. It is the journey toward self-discovery, embracing one's true calling and living it with authenticity and dedication.

3. **MOKSHA**, often described as the ultimate liberation or freedom from the cycles of rebirth, is attained through spiritual enlightenment and self-realization. It represents the journey toward understanding one's true self and experiencing unity with the divine.

Aava

4. **BRAHMAN**, in the Vedic tradition, is often described as the ultimate reality or cosmic principle. It is viewed as the supreme and universal consciousness or energy that underlies all of existence. Brahman is the source and essence of everything, and realization of brahman is a key aspect of spiritual enlightenment in many Indian philosophies.

5. **ATMAN**, the individual soul or self, represents the essence of an individual beyond their physical existence.

The journey of yoga and meditation provides pathways to transcend the limitations of the physical body and expand the mind. Through these practices, individuals can attain higher states of consciousness and connect with atman, their eternal self. It is a profound journey of self-discovery and inner realization that leads to greater spiritual depth and understanding. I always felt a deep connection to India's principles of philosophy and to its revered sages and their teachings. India's rich spiritual heritage has directly influenced many seekers on their journeys of self-discovery and inner growth, serving as a source of inspiration and guidance on the path to a greater spiritual understanding.

Maharishi Mahesh Yogi's teachings of Transcendental Meditation, Vedic philosophy, and the science of Ayurveda have been instrumental on my journey. His wisdom and guidance in these practices have provided me invaluable support, offering pathways to deeper self-discovery, spiritual growth, and holistic well-being. Gratitude comes from my heart for Maharishi's teachings and enlightened presence, an acknowledgment of the profound impact he had on shaping my path and nurturing my personal transformation.

THE DIVINITY OF NATURE

I wander along a nature trail, meandering through forests and fields and alongside rivers. These sacred places provide me with sustenance. I absorb life through the very air I breathe; it infuses my essence with vitality. The lush greenery of the trees and leaves, the harmonious songs of the birds, and the restful presence of wildlife exude a vibrant spiritual energy. Within nature's

embrace I find a sanctuary that invokes feelings of divinity, where the sacred and natural world merge in perfect harmony.

Gaia, in Greek mythology, is the personification of the Earth itself. She is considered one of the primordial deities and is often referred to as the mother goddess. Gaia emerged at the beginning of creation, born from chaos, and she gave birth to Titans, Cyclops, and other significant beings in Greek mythology. In my perception, Gaia is the very essence of life on Earth. She intricately weaves herself into the creation of the world and cosmos, nurturing the Earth's fertility and abundance. Gaia embodies the Earth itself, radiating its beauty and vitality and the interconnectedness of all life on our planet. Preserving the natural world, and honoring Gaia's sacred role in sustaining life, is our duty and responsibility.

THE SACREDNESS OF BANYAN TREES

I am walking beneath the great banyan trees in Bangkok, experiencing the splendor of Thailand and encountering symbols of eternal life and immortality. These majestic trees stand as a timeless witness to the country's rich cultural and spiritual heritage. The banyan tree's long lifespan and continuous growth evoke a cyclical pattern of existence, and its multiple trunks and intertwining branches represent the complex journey of spiritual growth and enlightenment. The deep roots of this tireless tree suggest a connection with the Earth and a sense of grounding. I perceive them as embodying stability and rootedness.

The streets of Bangkok hold within them a striking revelation: the coexistence and interdependence of the new and the old. This realization unfolds as the vibrant cityscape seamlessly weaves together modernity and tradition—towering skyscrapers with ancient temples, sleek malls with vibrant markets—symbolizing a harmonious blend in which the old enriches the new and the new embraces the essence of the old. Bangkok stands as a living testament to the notion that progress and innovation thrive upon the foundation laid by tradition and heritage.

Thai spirituality is traditionally rooted in Buddhism and emphasizes compassion, kindness, generosity, mindfulness, and the inevitability of the law of karma.

Meditation holds a significant place in Thai culture. It is deeply ingrained in the lives of Thai people as a core practice for various reasons, including as a spiritual tradition, to cultivate mindfulness, to reduce stress, and to attain inner peace. Meditation is seen as a way to achieve mental clarity and emotional balance in daily life.

BALI'S RICH SPIRITUAL TRADITIONS

Bali is often referred to as the "Island of the Gods" and is known for its joyful and enchanting atmosphere. Its breathtaking natural beauty, vibrant culture, warm-hearted people, and spiritual aura make it a destination that captivates the heart of many travelers. Bali has a unique charm that is hard to resist. It is a place where one can find happiness, peace, and a deeper connection to inner and outer worlds.

As I walk around, I see villages filled with temples, shrines, and holy sites. These places are spiritual sanctuaries where locals and visitors can connect with themselves and the divine. The collective consciousness in Bali is a blend of spirituality, community values, cultural heritage, and an appreciation for the interconnectedness of life. With its unique identity and nurturing environment, Bali has a special way of fostering a sense of unity among its people. It invites individuals from all walks of life to explore and deepen their spiritual journeys.

Balinese people hold strong spiritual beliefs, practicing a unique form of Hinduism that is intertwined with their daily lives. Their deep connection to religion is reflected in the ceremonies, rituals, and offerings that are an integral part of their culture. Balinese Hinduism is a blend of Hindu, Buddhist, and indigenous Balinese beliefs that creates a rich fabric of spiritual practices that make Bali an enriching and captivating place to visit.

THE INTERCONNECTEDNESS OF EAST AND WEST

The philosophies of both Eastern and Western traditions exhibit incredible diversity and variation within their ideologies. Within each tradition exist

diverse perspectives, beliefs, and interpretations that offer a fascinating array of insights and approaches to comprehend life, existence, and the human experience. This diversity enriches our understanding of the world and provides different paths for individuals to explore and connect with their own spiritual or philosophical beliefs. It is a testament to the richness of human thought and the many ways we seek to make sense of the complexity of existence.

Western philosophy is rooted in rational inquiry, critical thinking, and the pursuit of knowledge through logical analysis and empirical observation. It emphasizes individualism, freedom, and the exploration of moral and ethical principles. It contrasts with Eastern philosophies, which encompass a deep reverence for interconnectedness, mindfulness, and inner peace. They engage in the quest for truth and meaning in human existence. Eastern teachings emphasize harmony with nature, the importance of balance, and the cultivation of wisdom through introspection and meditation. Central themes include the impermanence of life, the concept of karma, and the belief in achieving enlightenment or self-realization through spiritual practice.

Journeys are more than just physical travels; they are passages to transformation. As I traversed the globe, each step echoed with new experiences and enlightening encounters, shaping my soul and enriching my understanding of the world and of myself. These voyages served both as a mirror, reflecting my inner growth, and as a white canvas on which I painted my life's experiences. The insights gained from these odysseys transcended mere sight-seeing; they restructured my perception, broadening the horizons of my mind. This immersion challenged the comfort of my known world, inviting me to question my beliefs and conditioning while embracing the differences that make up our world.

Each journey became an opportunity to explore external and internal landscapes, providing a deeper understanding of the connection of all beings. The exchange of ideas, the shared laughter, and the moments of connection with the locals resonated most deeply within me. It was in these moments of human contact that I felt the true essence of my travels, transcending borders and language to touch the heart of our shared humanity.

With a camera in hand, I embarked on a journey that went beyond mere snapshots. Through the lens, I discovered a way to connect with nature on a deeper level, capturing the beauty of the world around me in a way that allowed me to see and appreciate its intricacy and wonders. My love of flowers shines through in my photographs. I enjoy capturing the precious essence of a flower's petals or the sprawling branches of an ancient tree. Each image becomes a celebration of the splendor and diversity found in nature, inviting me to appreciate the marvels surrounding me. Photography became my new language—an unspoken dialogue with nature, as I immersed myself in each moment, feeling the pulse of life in every frame.

Sharing my captured moments alongside my thoughts and memories is an invitation for others to step into themselves, into the emotions and experiences woven into each photograph. Each image became a doorway, a portal, through which I could share my stories and sentiments, creating a deeper connection between the viewer and the moment I had witnessed and captured. Art takes me away from the ordinary aspects of life; it elevates my mind and emotions, revealing a broader view of myself and the world. As Oscar Wilde once said, *"Art is the most intense mode of individualism the world has known."* This phrase is a beautiful reminder of how art can touch our souls and allow us to express our individuality.

Marcel Proust beautifully expressed it in saying, *"Through art, we can get outside of ourselves and know another's view of the universe."* Artists have a remarkable ability to transport me beyond my own perspective and connect me with different dimensions of the world. Their creative expressions, born from their experiences, visions, and energies, have the power to make me feel better; they inspire me and evoke emotions that resonate deep within me. Art has the remarkable ability to enrich our lives and broaden our understanding of human experience.

PART II
THE TAPESTRY OF MY LIFE

UNVEILING MY INNER CHILD

> In the vast kingdom of my heart lived a gentle soul, whose deepest desire was to be nurtured with the gift of freedom.
>
> In my quest for freedom, the path was not without its thorns. I often found myself navigating through the dense, shadowy forest of my own fears, insecurities, and doubts.
>
> These were not ordinary fears; they were rooted in caution and restraint, weaving an invisible web that threatened to prevent my inner child from dancing freely in the meadows of her imagination and exploration.

In the tender innocence of youth, little Claudia, my inner child, is nestled, yearning for protection from life's uncertain tides. Yet, in my deepest desire to shield her, I inadvertently hindered her from embracing the beauty of her own journey. In moments of reflection, I realized how life's constraints had formed a tight cocoon around her, limiting her ability to spread her wings and embrace life fully, leaving scars upon her soul. Her deepest desire was a simple profound wish: to find solace in the gentle embrace of unconditional love.

For many years she felt lifeless, sad, and frustrated; her voice was muffled. She felt alone and hid from people, always shy and afraid of expressing herself and not being understood. She remained concealed in the shadows of her soul, unaware of the radiant light dwelling within. Her vulnerability, emerging from the depth of being, became a conduit for me to connect with her voice.

This gentle aspect of my inner child intertwined with my adult self, creating a seamless fabric woven with emotions and experiences. Growing up brought conflicting challenges that made me question my identity many times, asking myself, "Who am I?" Sensitivity clashed with courage, curiosity danced with vulnerability, while independence wrestled against responsibility, creating a complex inner landscape shaped by those opposing forces.

At my core, I embrace an innate openness to my intuition, eagerly seeking the elusive key that unlocks the mysteries of my deepest self. It has been an endless exploration, taking countless years to truly grasp and embrace my roots, to unravel the intricate threads of my lineage. A lifetime pursuit led me to inner peace.

In my quest, I discovered that what I sought to grasp externally lay within the depths of my inner space, in a realm brimming with visions, thoughts, secrets, and truths waiting to be revealed. It was during this inward journey that I found the peace, harmony, joy, and fulfillment that I was looking for.

Writing my story transcends the mere act of storytelling. It is an endeavor to retrace the roots of my spiritual and physical lineage, roots that extend far beyond the tangible soil to which I belong. It is an examination of the interconnectedness of my past, my essence, and the very foundation from which I have originated.

I grew up in a strict and disciplined environment shaped by my parents' outlook and upbringing. I had deep love and respect for my parents. My father embodied a multitude of strengths—he had a warrior spirit driven by vision, clarity, unwavering determination, and stability. Sometimes emotionally unavailable, constantly pioneering new paths, he was determined and unyielding, not afraid to push boundaries or challenge the status quo. My mother possessed a resilient and beautiful spirit, yet was often overshadowed by my father. Her struggles added depth and complexity to her character. Both of my parents were authentic and deeply rooted in their tradition and values. They were loving and caring parents to their five children. I felt the strength of our family bond and the significance of our lineage.

As a child, the beach held a special place in my heart. It was more than just a picturesque location; it was a haven of solace and contemplation. I could immerse myself in introspection, letting the soothing sounds of the waves and the vast ocean inspire my thoughts and nourish my soul. The perpetual movement of the tides reminds me of life's cycles—ebb and flow, beginnings and endings.

From the shore that withstands the relentless force of the waves, I learn resilience. The murmur of the sea invites me to be present in the moment.

Cavafy's poignant poem "Ithaka" became a treasured discovery later in my life. It is a metaphoric exploration of life's journey and the importance of that journey itself, rather than the destination. Cavafy always encourages his readers to savor life's teachings, its challenges, and the personal growth encountered along the way. His message is that the true value of life lies in the quest and the wisdom gained from it, rather than solely in reaching a specific goal. He inspires me to embrace life's adventures, to learn from my experiences, and find fulfillment in the process of self-discovery.

Amid of the world's chaos, I often felt like a soul confined, yearning to rediscover my essence and seek solace. Thus began my soul's odyssey, a quest for reconnection and remembrance. My journey started with the longing for a place I considered home. I learned to listen to the whispers of the wind and the gentle rustle of leaves, understanding the silent language of my own heart along the way.
I meditated under the stars, looking for comfort in the tranquility of the night. The universe revealed its mysteries, igniting a flicker of self-awareness within.

In misty mountains and rolling hills, my soul encountered trials, and I found myself confronting shadows hiding within. Each challenge became a mirror of concealed fears and dormant strengths. Through introspection, my soul unravels layers of conditioning and societal expectations that shaped me. By peeling away these layers and masks, I move toward a more authentic self, a core self that exists beneath the external influences and pressures. This process of embracing authenticity is both liberating and challenging, as it often involves confronting uncomfortable truths about myself and the world around me. It is really a path toward living more genuinely and fully aligning my actions and beliefs with my true self.

This pilgrimage of self-discovery led my soul beyond the bustling cities to sacred temples and hallowed grounds. In these serene spiritual sanctuaries, gurus and mentors imparted ancient teachings, offering knowledge that has been preserved and passed down through generations. These teachings honor traditions, provide deep insights and guidance and illuminate the path toward inner peace and enlightenment. I embrace the teachings and experiences of the sacred places to reach the eternal wisdom that transcends the cycles of time. Among ancient echoes and modern yearnings, I discover that true knowledge and comprehension flow freely, unbound by the constraints of time or place. They wait for those who seek with open hearts, ready to reveal the way to authenticity and enlightenment.

The journey of self-reconnection is not about reaching a fixed destination, but embracing the ever-unfolding evolution of being. It is akin to a pilgrimage, a perpetual dance between the realms of the known and unknown. In this delicate balance, each step forward becomes a sacred movement toward growth and self-discovery. My soul reemerges, healed and renewed, adorned with the jewels of insight and inner guidance. With each fragment mended, I awaken to a higher plane of awareness, embracing a deeper understanding of my purpose and place in the world.

True spirituality is a captivating journey of compassion, inner peace, love, unity, and the pursuit of higher consciousness. It gifts us with the virtues of letting go, detachment, and surrender, allowing us to create space within ourselves to coexist with the mystical wonders of the universe. The practice of letting go is akin to a fairy's gift, bestowing upon me the beauty of releasing attachments and freeing my spirit from burdens. Through detachment, I find the clarity to observe life with a serene gaze, going beyond the need to control. In surrender, my soul transcends, soaring on the wings of eternity. It is a humbling lesson, learning to embrace the impermanence of the physical realm, while nurturing the eternal flame that flickers within.

As I reconnect with my true essence, my self-love blossoms. It gently peels away the layers of old conditioning and programming, revealing the radiant core of my being. In these intimate bonds, I unearth the authentic wellspring of love, cultivating a deep reservoir of appreciation and kindness toward myself, like the gentle magic of fairies in a hidden vale. In the realm of self-love, I honor, respect, and accept every facet of myself—strengths and weaknesses, virtues

and imperfections, nurturing a sense of self-worth and inner tranquility. I weave protective boundaries to safeguard my well-being. Living in harmony with my values and beliefs, I bask in the radiance of each moment and my heart overflows with gratitude.

> **One day in New York, as I reorganized my closet, Jesus surprised me. His peaceful presence and gaze penetrated my being. Seeing deep into my soul, he shared a transformative truth: "From this day forward, you are my student. I am here by your side. Ask me questions, share your doubts and fears. I will always support you through both challenges and gentle times, guiding and inspiring you on this healing journey you've begun."**
>
> **It took me a few seconds to center myself. In that fleeting moment, I was engulfed by waves of panic, oblivious to the significance of his words. Fear gripped my heart, and for a breathless instant I thought my life was ending.**
>
> **Yet, in the stillness that followed, I found my center, a tranquil, serene feeling. His gentle voice, imbued with love and wisdom, left an indelible mark on my soul. This transformative moment planted seeds for my inward journey.**

As the years passed, weaving threads of experiences and introspection, this enigmatic divine encounter began to unveil its hidden depths. With each meditation and the gentle guidance of metaphysical teachings, the veils of forgetfulness and ignorance started lifting, revealing the wisdom nestled within Jesus' words.

His revelation echoed through the chambers of my soul, resonating with a truth long dormant, awakening a deep desire to unfold the petals of my true self, to shine forth with authenticity and purity that had been shrouded in shadow for so long. The divine encounter with Jesus came at a pivotal juncture in my life's journey, as I embarked on a new chapter in New York, far from the embrace of family.

Today, I realize that Brazil represents my roots because it embodies the essence of my lineage, culture, tradition, and was the foundation of my identity.

New York offers me space and freedom for my spiritual development. It is a dynamic and diverse environment, providing opportunities for growth, introspection, and learning. It became a vast canvas for my spiritual exploration and personal transformation.

My connection to Jesus transcends the confines of religion and resonates as an archetype of love and forgiveness. Jesus symbolizes timeless virtues that move beyond cultural and religious boundaries. His archetype speaks to all of us as a guiding light, a teacher of love and compassion, emphasizing the inherent human capacity for empathy and redemption.

FOLLOWING MY BLISS

In the dance of existence, conflict births life's symphony,
War entwined with peace, pain, embraced by bliss.
Hatred entangled with compassion's gentle kiss.
Amid these dueling forces, I find my harmony,
The melody of my truth, a soul's sweet daydream
Like a wise fool, innocent guide,
I rejoice in love, light, inner joy!
Imagination is the golden compass of my soul's wide sea.

Over time, I drifted away from my true nature, losing touch with the inner wisdom that once guided me. I wanted to fit in, but it was not comfortable, and I did not see my reality reflected anywhere around me. I sought inspiration and fulfillment outside myself, yearning for people, stories, and concepts to lead me toward deeper happiness and contentment.

As I came across the wisdom of wizards, magicians, seers, shamans, and gurus, figures that have existed throughout time in deep forests, silent caves, and sacred temples, I gained words to name and express the experience of my higher

self. I recognized something very familiar and natural. Wizards, magicians, and healers are capable of perceiving vulnerabilities and discerning the root causes of suffering. The knowledge of metaphysical principles they share guided me in self-empowerment and mastery of my life.

The higher self perceives the world as a grand illusion, a manifestation of consciousness in motion. Connecting to my deeper truth clarifies my past experiences and conditioning, revealing new insights.

Through the wisdom of my inner guidance and insights from my teachers, I grasp the importance of disciplining and mastering my mind, strengthening my inner chi—the vital energy inherent in all living beings. As I connect with my higher self, my life flows effortlessly, and I feel aligned with my path. I sense the support of the universe in every step I take as it reveals the magic of synchronicity.

Deepak Chopra describes that *"life unfolds through a series of spontaneous synchronicities, always surprising us along the way. The voice of the wise one becomes clearer as the heart heals, and innocence returns, which is our natural state of being. The wizard remains undistracted by the voice of the ego. At its core, the essence of the wizard is transformation."*

The concept of wisdom is deeply ingrained in mythology and folklore, as well as embodied in figures such as Merlin in the tales of King Arthur, who serves as an adviser and counselor. Similarly, in Homer's epic *The Odyssey*, the goddess Athena graces Odysseus' destiny with wisdom, guidance, and transformation.

The archetype of the wise and mystical guide appears in various forms and can shapeshift as needed, inspiring us with eternal messages across different cultures and time periods. The various forms meet the universal human need to pursue greater knowledge and inner change.

Merlin's advice to the young Arthur entails the art of transforming self-imposed limitations into the mastery of infinite possibilities, so he can achieve love, fulfillment, and spiritual connection.

Athena's message to Odysseus emphasizes the importance of the right intellect, perseverance, resourcefulness, and honor in overcoming challenges and achieving his goals. Athena's guidance and support play a crucial role in Odysseus' journey and eventual return to Ithaca.

The so-called wizard, the inner teacher, is not someone who attempts alchemy or falls in love, because he is already permanently in the flow of love, always guiding us toward becoming free and loving individuals.

Jesus, Buddha, and Muhammad were revered spiritual teachers who transmitted wisdom and teachings centered upon love, compassion, and transformation, much like the concept of the inner teacher or wizard. They left a lasting legacy of spiritual guidance for humanity.

In my personal journey as a Catholic woman, realizing that the true kingdom of heaven resides within me was deeply transformational. This realization made me understand the significance of inner work, which includes clearing away emotional barriers and illusions to nurture spiritual growth and forge a deeper connection to the divine within.

In a state of openness and contemplation, my inner wizard is the loving ever-presence that offers answers and guidance whenever I seek them. He is always reminding me, *"Don't take life so seriously,"* as he playfully scampers around me along my path, through a green magical field.

My wizard fills me with energy and mirth, much like Dorothy's journey in *The Wizard of Oz* brings her moments of inspiration and growth. Throughout her adventures in the magical land of Oz, Dorothy encounters various characters and situations that symbolize different aspects of her own desires and fears. The central theme is that the power to achieve one's goals and overcome challenges

often lies within. Ultimately, Dorothy gains the ability to return home by believing in herself. Through the support of her own inner courage, perseverance, and many friends, she overcomes her challenges and conquers her destiny. Along the way, she learns about the importance of self-love.

I have crossed the threshold into a new phase of life. The horizon stretches before me, painted with hues of hope and possibility. Each step forward leads me closer to the promise of a brighter future, where dreams wait patiently to be realized. In my hero's odyssey, inspired by the wisdom of Joseph Campbell, I have come to realize that my quest for home transcends mere geography. It is not about returning to a specific physical location, but rather about finding a state of being—a deep sense of fulfillment nestled in the chambers of my heart. It is a journey inward, a sacred pilgrimage toward the essence of my true self, where I find the ultimate meaning of belonging and wholeness. I hear a gentle voice urging me onward, nurturing my spiritual growth with each step I take.

My commitment to myself is unwavering—I plant the seeds of my visions, cultivating the qualities of being that have long danced in the realms of my dreams. With each intention set and every action taken, the radiant potential of my truest self blossoms into the fullest expression of who I am meant to be. Walking on the beach, gazing at the blue sky, I reflect upon Maharishi's words:

"We do not acquire happiness.
Our very nature is happiness.
Bliss is not newly earned.
All that needs to be done is to remove unhappiness."

THE SEED OF CONSCIOUSNESS

> **As I strolled along the beach amid the tranquil sound of waves, with sand between my toes and the horizon ablaze in hues of amber, a whisper stirred within me: "You should buy a studio." I questioned the voice, and it responded, "Return to life's sacred classroom, but take it seriously. Honor the teachings with steadfast dedication."**

Guided by an inner call, I acquired a modest studio close to my home, even though its purpose was shrouded in enigma. Little did I know that within those humble walls a sacred pilgrimage would unfold—a journey of self-discovery and spiritual awakening, where every moment spent became a step closer to the essence of my being. Awakened to my passions, I embark on sculpting my heart's desires into an inner marble block. My muse, the embodiment of my true nature, flows gracefully to the rhythm of its own melody.

My quest unfolds as a lifetime adventure, guided by a profound yearning for love. Delving deep within myself, I seek the source of this hunger, ultimately reconnecting with the essence of who I am. In this sacred exploration, I unearth the infinite wellspring of self-love within, a love that transcends the limitations of human nature.

Transcendental love is anchored in a spiritual bond that surpasses mere desires, emotional attachments, and the trappings of codependency often found in relationships. It is a love that compels me to fully embrace myself and infuses my life with purpose and meaning, connecting me to something greater than myself. This ideal love is like a seismic attraction, an embrace that changes the course of life.

I travel through time and space in search of my missing half, longing to become whole again. Eventually, I come to realize that what I yearn for exists within me. I need not seek it in others. This marks an awakening, a newfound recognition of my spiritual truth. As Ralph Waldo Emerson once aptly put it, *"Life is a journey, not a destination."*

In the depths of my heart, I envision the eagle, a powerful symbol of hope, freedom, and peace. I am reminded of the words of Martin Luther King, Jr., *"We must accept finite disappointment, but never lose infinite hope."*

I am on a quest to unravel the meaning of life, which has been encoded within us since our earliest days in human form. The disconnection I feel is a universal theme, outlined in the story of Adam and Eve in the Garden of Eden. The fall from Paradise, with which we were both blessed and cursed, marks the end of our experience of eternity, a facet of our original nature. This is the beginning of duality and the illusions of the relative world. I sense disconnection from source, prompting me to embark on a quest for the root of knowledge. I seek answers to fundamental questions: "Who created life? Who created death?"

The world unfolds from a dream, a dream woven into myths. Within this mythic realm, the dichotomies of good and evil, Adam and Eve, reality and imagination, life and death, dance in an intricate tapestry of existence. As I journey farther along my path, I sense fragments, myriad facets, and lurking shadows. These shadows, as Carl Jung proclaimed, harbor the dark side within us that is rooted in the collective history of humanity. They reside in the depths of the collective unconscious, housing bubbles of beliefs, experiences, and ideas accumulated over time. Even in the face of intense inner and outer battles, a flame flickers within me. My heart offers glimpses of hope and trust, assuring me that one day victory will be mine.

> **I have felt the weight of tradition, the echoes of history reverberating through my being.**
> **Amid it all, I hear the singular heroic voice calling out.**
> **I yearn to dance, to flow, to merge, with the rhythm of existence.**
> **In this symphony of life, I sense the tragedy, the dignity, the sorrow and the boundless compassion.**
> **As I surrender to the melody of nature, I fall into love, into oneness with all that is.**

This is the story of myself, the path of my destiny. I am returning to my genuine nature, saluting all weaknesses and virtues of myself. My mind reaches out to grasp the vastness of universal truth, seeking to expand beyond the confines of the known. My body yearns for vitality and vigor, to be a proper vessel through which to manifest my highest aspirations. And from deep within, my spirit wants to soar, to break free from the shackles of doubt and fear, and to trust wholeheartedly in the visions that guide me.

I entered this world, my heart brimming with dreams, each one a secret passion, waiting to take flight like birds released from their cage. I am the hero of my own story, destined to chase dreams of love, joy, adventure, and fulfillment until they become my reality.

PART III
VISIONS ALONG THE PATH

AN OPEN HEART

My visions are bestowed upon me from higher realms of imagination, offering glimpses into aspects of myself that are waiting to be realized. They are expressions of a heightened state of consciousness, reflecting what I aspire to become. Each vision illuminates my future self, guiding me toward self-realization and happiness. They serve as challenges, urging me to grow, expand, and explore new horizons. Through their inspiration, I reconnect with my true self, fostering innermost qualities that lead to fulfillment.

> **As I meditate, I envision myself embodying the essence of a teenage peasant girl, a symbolic messenger from my true nature that urges me to reconnect with the natural world. Clad in a long linen frock layered beneath a sleeveless tunic, with a scarf gracefully draped over her head and leather boots snugly laced around her ankles, she epitomizes a serene and harmonious lifestyle full of nature's beauty. Surrounding her are beautiful trees, vibrant flowers, and crystalline blue waters, evoking a sense of tranquility and connectedness to the Earth.**

The peasant girl emerges as a seeker of light. She yearns for happiness and fulfillment and embarks on a quest for her ideal. Driven by a deep longing to venture beyond the confines of tradition, she is guided by the wisdom of her heart and the innate knowing of her soul. With a fervent desire to manifest her truest essence, she follows the path of her destiny.

My journey unfolds with the excitement of revelation as I explore the mysteries of life and awaken mystical dimensions within myself. Each step leads me closer to a deeper understanding of my true essence and purpose.

> **A large, sturdy white daisy emerges from the earth and takes root in my heart, symbolizing a deep longing within my soul to reconnect and find home within.**

However, I notice that the dahlia turns away from me, expressing anger and frustration. It communicates that my thoughts and emotions are hindering its ability to fully manifest and experience earthly existence. I feel trapped within myself.

As I dive deeper into myself, I encounter a magnificent sturdy tree, symbolizing future possibilities. Floating within its robust trunk, I feel a stream of energy, my life-force, flowing through my body. Emerging from this experience in a lotus position, I smile radiantly, suffused with inner tranquility and joy.

However, as I return to the surface and open my eyes I am confronted by a massive cloud made of thoughts and realize their dominance over my spirit. In the search for my source, fear grips my heart, rendering it frozen and unable to find connection. A thin veil of long threads obscures my vision, deepening the pain of disconnection. My genuine self shatters into fragments, each representing a facet of my personality, fueled by their own energy and intensity, they paint the canvas of my life. They appear as monstrous figures, taking on various forms, each representing challenges to overcome.

A mysterious witch, her body contorted by fear, is lurking in shadows.
A dwarf, burned by life's struggles, is clenched in a martyr's stance.
A nun, stifling her instincts, veiling her passions beneath a spiritual mask, is haunted by a fear of God and authority.
A madwoman, dwelling in a dilapidated house, consumed by dust, is suppressing her inner strength, until rebellion stirs within her.

Encountering the devil, the embodiment of fear, I hear his words echo …."It is all a waste of time." With those words, direction dissipates, and I feel the collapse of my imagination.

Before me glides a regal lion, its mane aglow with the shimmer of gold. Its fiery gaze, ablaze with crimson, exudes passion, desire, and fierce determination.

The wizard arrives like an eagle, gracefully descending into a serene, tranquil meadow, casting a vision of hope for the future.

A mystical dragon with gleaming, piercing eyes surges within me, fervently endeavoring to rouse me from my complete numbness. His movements are fierce, a testament to his yearning for liberation, as he struggles to unleash his fiery essence.
The dragon is my spirit's flame.

Each fragment is manifested in a different shape, like characters of a fairy tale interwoven in the fabric of my life. The nun, the fairy, the dwarf, and the wizard spoke to me and inspired me, as intangible friends that urged me to embrace my imagination and listen to the wisdom of my consciousness. The experience of light, colors, and textures is the excitement and beauty of creation.

A fairy gently alights and caresses my heart with her delicate touch. Instantly, a profound sense of peace washes over me and my entire being relaxes, surrendering to the tranquility she brings.

A delicate woman, mirroring the scars of a disconnected warrior, appears before me. Inside, the myriad voices take on extraordinary forms, each asserting its dominance with wild fervor, echoing loudly in the depths of my being.

When my mind is imbued with positivity, my imagination ascends to lofty realms, enveloped by the presence of luminous beings like fairies and angels. However, in the grip of negative thoughts and memories, my vibrational frequency diminishes, drawing me into a realm of shadowy figures, monsters, and witches, formed by a mind constricted by fear and a heart sealed shut. Visions grace me when I am deeply connected to my pure mind, and my heart is open wide. In these moments, I am inspired to fully embrace life, to heal, and to integrate the wisdom of my visions into every fiber of my being.

An open heart serves as a vital conduit to heightened happiness, success, and joy. It is the miraculous elixir that heals, provides clarity, and unlocks the doors of my inner confinement. I step into my future guided by the wisdom and strength within. In this state of consciousness, I feel the heartbeat of the universe, resonating with the harmony and enchantment of existence. Such enlightenment dawns when we are receptive, listening with our hearts instead of our heads. Our reality transforms into a gentler, more nurturing environment ripe for personal evolution and expansion.

In the depth of my being, I yearn for tranquility, where the formless gives birth to new experiences, and consciousness flourishes in its purest essence. In this sacred space, I am enveloped by the radiant flames of newfound awareness akin to the blaze of divine wisdom. Here, I draw nearer to the source, on the threshold of profound transformation. My perception widens and life unfolds with graceful simplicity.

RECONNECTING WITH MY TRUE NATURE

I am walking on the beach in the early morning. I feel constriction in my heart.

> **Luckily, in spite of being entangled in this profound internal and external battle I see a tender, very loving white hand knocking on my heart and I hear a whisper.... "Open up.... Open up.... You forgot who you are."**

When I lose touch with stillness, I lose myself. A strong desire to reach my core energy grows inside of me. I plunge into subtle levels of unconscious and subconscious memories. I touch the cosmic mind. I have spiritual experiences, insights, visions, guidance, and revelation. It is the beginning of my awakening and my spiritual reconnection. I am learning to navigate from a state of numbness to one of conscious living. This process of awakening leads me to observe, surrender, and practice ego relaxation. Surrendering to my heart is a practice that takes me from outer turmoil to inner peace. My transformative journey leads me to a straight path filled with mystery and magic. It awakens the mystical dimensions of myself.

We ourselves are the mystery we seek to know! We are always looking for a deeper experience of life. The way I see it, every god or goddess reflects the imperfect and whimsical traits of humanity. As our consciousness evolves, we ought to break free of the past and welcome our future. The secret to creating our future is living in the present, from our higher mind, which allows our consciousness to expand, acquire new insights, and attract new opportunities.

Love is the highest, most beautiful, and deepest feeling there is. It is the expression of spiritual evolution. It takes courage to love, and it takes courage to be loved. Love reconciles the masculine and feminine elements that coexist inside of me. Truth is love, and all the rest is an illusion. Passion is what triggers love into action, the fire that urges me to express who I really am. Evolution is about aligning myself with the mystery of my future.

A hidden destiny is waiting to be discovered within the vast realms of possibilities. In my life's new chapter, I set sail guided by the gentle touch of love, the radiant light of understanding, and the joyful melody of inner peace. Along this journey, enlightenment unfolds, blossoms, and is nurtured by self-awareness and the introspective gaze into the mirror of my soul.

The purest nectar of the heart is love, an all-embracing love that nurtures the self with joy and bliss, and gives us the energy to expand and blossom like flowers. In the ancient Chinese text *Tao Te Ching*, the sage Lao-Tzu offers some words of wisdom about the process of reconnecting with our true nature:

"Become totally empty,
Quiet the restlessness of the mind.
Only then will you witness everything...
A mind free of thought,
merged within itself
beholds the essence of Tao
A mind filled with thought,
identified with its own perceptions,
beholds the mere forms of this world...
See all things flourish and dance

in endless variations,
And once again merge back into perfect emptiness—
Their true repose,
Their true nature
Emerging, flourishing, dissolving back again.
This is the eternal process of return.
To know this process brings enlightenment...
A vision of oneness brings about universal love
Universal love supports the great truth of Nature."

—VERSES 1 AND 16, TRANSLATED BY JONATHAN STAR

THE GIFT OF LIFE

During my meditation, I am surprised by a lady with golden hair and shimmering eyes.
The fairy, radiant and pure, reaches into the depths of my heart, sweeping away the accumulated gloom and lethargy.
She engulfs me in waves of love and showers me with pink bubbles of innocence.
The lady bestows upon me the precious gift of consciousness, the essence of unbounded devotion, and unveils the destiny and purpose of my emerging self.
With her shimmering gaze fixed upon me, her pristine voice soars into my heart, "Life is a gift, and our legacy is to live it fully, to be embraced by its beauty." Filled with gratitude, I thank her.
I draw closer to her, ready to embrace the wonders of this newfound awareness.
Twice, I extend my arms to embrace her, but both times, my hands grasp nothing but air.
The fairy resembles a muse, ethereal and devoid of earthly trappings.
Her mere presence leaves me in awe. Curiosity grips me and I ask:
"Are you divine or mortal? Have you ever tasted the sweetness of an apple or felt the warmth of a lover's hug?"

With a serene smile she replies, "We are not cut from the same cloth. My existence is divine, sustained by the nectar of the gods." Her words leave me incredulous, prompting me to lean forward in an attempt to test if she is real with a pinch.
Once more, she smiles and explains, "Pinching me is like pinching a cloud. I am as benevolent as a guardian angel. You can see me, but you can't touch me."

As she captivates me with her strength and words, she vanishes beyond the rainbow's end, into a land of unimaginable dreams and infinite possibilities. She is gone to a place unknown to me, where she belongs in heavenly eternity.

This remarkable encounter with the lady of the golden hair and shimmering eyes has brought me to the ethereal realms of existence.

FORGING PATHS

On a radiant day, basking in the sun's warmth, I wander along the shoreline, capturing snapshots of footprints imprinted in the white sand—a testament to a solitary voyager pondering life's mysteries. As the wise Lao-Tzu once said, *"The journey of a thousand miles begins with a single step."*

How do paths begin? Where do they start? Where do my inner guides and facets spring from? Paths begin with the sparkle of evening stars, painting the sky with their radiant light, igniting a sense of excitement and wonder in every step.

In the depths of darkness, there resides a gentle glow. My journey through the night is never as obscure as it may appear. Within the silence, there is solace, and amid the quietude, whispers of inspiration and guidance gently reach out to me, illuminating my path forward.

I observe. Setting goals gives my life direction. It boosts my motivation and self-confidence. I am following my visions. Every day fulfills its purpose. My actions reinforce my goals. The knowledge of my weaknesses and strengths sustains my talents and ambitions. I am about to embark on a personal journey in search of knowledge and spirituality. It all depends upon my effort and commitment. My life path lies ahead as a road waiting to be traveled. It holds opportunities and challenges. It awakens my determination to embrace them.

In the silence of my meditation sessions, I find the most inspiring moments of my day. I have embraced Transcendental Meditation, a practice taught by Maharishi Mahesh Yogi, from India. It is a very simple, natural, and effortless technique. I sit down on my bed. I close my eyes. I take a few deep breaths and use the mantra to plunge into myself. I clear my mind, calm my emotions, and focus my attention. My shadowy fragments are brought back into alignment. In deep introspection, I confront the perennial question: Who am I?

In my mind's eye, I become a brave warrior
riding a white stallion, holding a sword made of silver.
Cutting the weeds on the path,
symbolizing the purification of my soul,
a journey of courage and self-control.

As I delve deeper within,
I stumble upon a grand marble statue,
an Egyptian deity, crumbling down.
As it fractures, it reveals a web of symbols,
encapsulating the essence of being.
A sacred script, in the language of my soul,
holding the blueprint of my purpose,
My destiny, and my divine connection.

THE UNION OF OPPOSITES

Within me resides a dichotomy: one part yearns to soar freely like a bird, while the other remains cocooned within a shell woven from past experiences and memories. As I navigate this intricate maze of emotions, I encounter the full

range of feelings. Once again, I find inspiration during my quiet moments, alone with my thoughts.

> **As I close my eyes, in the sanctuary of my heart's mind, the wise woman breaks her silence. Gesturing for me to sit beside her, she asks with a loving and gentle voice, "How are you my dear?"**
> **In a voice tinged with confusion and exasperation, I respond: "I am puzzled, frustrated, feeling powerless. Within me, myriad voices echo, a chorus of divergent sounds and messages buzzing inside my head."**
>
> **I sense the looming shadow of fear and negativity,**
> **embodied in a towering witch.**
> **She rides the winds on her broomstick,**
> **clad in a black cloak and pointed hat.**
> **Her inner murmur suggests a reluctance to venture**
> **into the unknown—deeming it all futile.**
>
> **Within me, conflicts stir, born of the ego's sway,**
> **An internal struggle unfolds, lingering, seeking its day.**
> **For the negative ego, fear is the guiding light,**
> **While the positive ego finds solace in love's might.**
>
> **In the quite sanctuary of my silent room, a vision unfolds—there stands the figure of a secret lover emerges before me, casting a gentle yet poignant presence.**
> **He is clad in a white shirt and black pants,a gentle yet poignant presence.**
> **I feel the man is caught in a tension between passion and spirituality, unable to embrace the sacredness of sex as a pure expression of cosmic energy.**

This vision offers a gentle invitation from within, guiding me to explore and embrace all hidden facets of myself.
It shows the split.
The forgotten truth.

We are spiritual beings having a human experience.
We were created from a divine blueprint.
Through sacred intimacy, two hearts deeply entwined can experience a direct connection to the divine, leading to a profound sense of self and a greater feeling of wholeness.

> **Where desire and spirituality merge, in the dance of life.**
> **It is the sacred union of soul and spirit, where feminine qualities, such as nurturing, compassion, and receptivity, meet masculine attributes like passion, strength, and fire.**
> **Together they create a balanced and integrated approach to life, allowing us to embody the best of both feminine and masculine energies.**
> **A mystical union, in harmony and grace,**
> **celebrating the balance, each finding their place.**
> **The union of opposites, leading to wholeness and fulfillment.**

My he-muse is naïve, eager, and noble. Like Don Quixote, he sees the world from a distinct angle, and each day brings a new adventure. Like Cervantes' aspiring knight-errant, my he-muse has faith in ideals. He gazes upward toward the endless sky as he goes, searching for clues from the universe. He is always surprised at the sight of new places, new horizons, new faces. He is traveling without much baggage, bearing just what is needed. He sees the light, feels the humor, and hears the laughter. He is stretching his imagination through his own soul. He holds in his hands a white rose. It reminds me how important it is to nurture a pure, positive mind and an innocent heart. A small white dog is always at his side, a symbol of loyalty, friendship, and devotion, always encouraging him to move forward and learn the lessons. There are mountains ahead, but he is aware of the challenges awaiting him on his travels. As Neem Karoli Baba says, *"Often one goes for one thing and finds another."*

In the middle of meditation, I find myself in a small, sparsely furnished room within the convent.

My surroundings slowly come into focus as the alarm interrupts my reverie. Pulling the thin comforter up to my neck, I become aware of my location. The room, though unadorned, exudes a sense of peace. I gaze out the large window overlooking the convent's backyard, and my attention is captured by a graceful seagull in flight. Its freedom resonates deep within my heart.

In the dim light around me, a mysterious shadow catches my attention.
I wonder if it is my imagination or a real presence.
As I focus, the figure becomes clearer—it is a nun, seemingly greeting me. This vision takes me back to a past life, where I lived as a nun.

Cloaked in the white cornette and traditional habit, the nun sits on a small hardwood chair.
Her eyes reveal a deep sense of fear, and she seems oblivious to the swirling black bats that hover around her, ominous and foreboding. Her appearance is haunting. She appears as if she is trapped in a vast bubble of dust.

Despite her dedication to a life of devotion and prayer to the Catholic God, there is hidden passion and a yearning for happiness and fulfillment beneath the surface.

Entangled in this intense inner and outer battle, she remains somewhat blind to her own truth. However, within her heart is a flickering flame that refuses to be extinguished. It provides her with a glimmer of hope and a sense of trust, assuring her that, someday, she will emerge victorious from this struggle.

I approach her and ask, "How are you feeling?"
She responds, "Like a fetus awaiting release from a mother's womb."
I can sense her fear of God and authority, which seems to paralyze her. She carries the heavy burden of tourmenting thoughts about the possibility of punishment.

She declares, "I gave my life to Him," her voice heavy with resentment and bitterness. Her gaze remains fixed in the distance. Then, as if in a trance, I witness a green window opening before her. A sense of mystery and a powerful presence envelop her. With newfound clarity, she rises from her foggy state and gradually vanishes. Though she is no longer visible, the lingering air seems to carry the weight of her resentment, akin to the chill of an autumn evening.

Women like the nun, spiritually confined by rigid religious beliefs, often struggle to recognize that the sweetness of life emerges from within, not solely from external sources.

Religion, known through an understanding of sacred texts and teachings, can sometimes inadvertently encourage the repression of emotions. However, true spirituality transcends mere rituals and dogma. It involves freeing our hearts from the grip of our subconscious mind, shedding the shadows, mist, and scars of past sorrows, ultimately liberating us to experience a deeper love and connection to the divine.

As I embrace spirituality, I become anchored in my heart, and the voice of an open heart is one of courage. As I dissolve into love, I tap into the experience of bliss, which is my ultimate gift. My greatest challenge is to fully embrace and live in alignment with my true nature.

Masters of both science and spirituality find common ground in the value of self-realization. Albert Einstein spoke about true religion, emphasizing that it involves living with one's whole soul.

The Dalai Lama shares a similar sentiment, believing that the only true religion is rooted in having a good heart. *"All love is directed toward the Self,"* Maharishi Mahesh Yogi explains.

THE MESSAGE OF A DAHLIA

In a mystical encounter with a dahlia, I am drawn into a world of hidden truths and unspoken messages. At first glance, the dahlia appears reserved, yet within its petals lies the essence of purity, love, and inner strength. As I study it closely, the vibrant petals seem to dance with intricate patterns and colors, each telling a unique story. I feel a connection to the wisdom this radiant bloom wishes to impart. Its message is clear: "Express your truest self," it whispers to my soul. The dahlia's vibrant colors and intricate patterns serve as a reminder that our uniqueness is a precious gift meant to be shared with the world. As the dahlia boldly displays its radiant petals, it encourages me to embrace my inner core and let my light shine brightly.

NAVIGATING THE DEPTHS OF MY SOUL

> **In the tender cradle of existence, I arrive with an open heart, a newborn eager to explore the tapestry of human experience. I sense I am on Earth to honor my soul's chosen path and to share the secrets of joy and love, weaving threads of connection and compassion.**
>
> **However, my self is concealed…. I see my life and story playing on the screen before me, and my infant self is in distress.**
>
> **I perceive a thin veil covering my eyes, camouflaging my true nature, disguising my truth. I find myself seriously absorbed in the game of life. I feel caged. I was meant to share my big blissful heart and unconditional love.**

In my journey of self-discovery, meditation has emerged as a cornerstone of

my mental well-being. It guides me on a profound voyage of self-transcendence, through which I gradually learn to embrace myself and the world with love and compassion.

In my life's earliest whispers, dreams found their home.
Each one a promise, a tale yet unknown.
Whispers of love, joy, of adventure untold.
In freedom's embrace, their stories unfold.
With the hero together, I seek skies to pursue,
In the dance of life, where dreams find their due.

In the passage of time, a conflict took seed within. My orthodox roots clashed with my spirit. Emotions swirled—anger, sadness, and frustration. A soul constrained, as if bound by walls, heart to heart, restricted, unable to fully express myself. Lost in the confines of tradition's hold, I yearned for freedom, a tale yet untold.

I embark on a journey that leads me through challenging experiences. Due to the constant fear of being hurt and the rise of anxiety, I created a barrier of self-protection to shield myself. This wall served as a defense mechanism to cope with the difficulties I encountered along the way. I faced struggles since I did not easily conform to traditions. I was strong enough and always have had the will to challenge norms and expectations, even in the face of difficulty. Thanks to the connection and guidance of my higher self, I've been able to face numerous challenges and embrace the lessons they offered. It was Einstein who famously said, *"No problem can be solved from the same level of consciousness that created it."* This quote underscores the importance of expanding our awareness and understanding in order to deal with our challenges effectively.

THE SEVEN FACES OF THE SOUL

The concept of "The Seven Faces of the Soul," as described by the spiritual guide Lazaris, refers to the different aspects or dimensions of human beings. These faces represent various facets of ourselves, each contributing to our overall essence and experience.

The soul is a living and vibrant being… and it is so much more. It has several specific faces, seven of them to be precise. Our soul is with us from the moment of birth to the moment of death and all the time in between. Each of its seven faces comes to us with many gifts. These gifts do not express themselves vocally, but rather come to us through our instinct and intuition. They come through the cracks and crevices of our life, in the silence and the stillness, and in the cherished moments.

When our heart is frozen the communication is broken. The heart holds the key. If we can hear the messages of the soul, so many answers will come, so many new directions can be found, and so much pain can be relieved and healed. There is so much magic if we can listen to our soul and know its faces.

1. THE NAME

In the context of "The Seven Faces of the Soul" the first face is "the name." Our name holds clues to our destiny, suggesting the significance of names and their connection to an individual's path in life. The name a person is given at birth carries inherent meaning related to their life purpose and journey. We bond to our parents and our family, but what we are really seeking is to bond with our soul. Lazaris emphasizes the importance of inner connection and self-awareness in navigating life's journey, suggesting that true fulfillment comes from aligning with one's authentic self and purpose.

2. POWER

The second face, "power," represents the stage in life when individuals begin to explore their ability to make choices, pursue their aspirations, and engage with the world around them. It implies a phase of realizing one's autonomy and capacity to influence one's own life and surroundings.

3. ETERNAL YOUTH

The third face of the soul, known as "eternal youth," is often symbolized by the element of fire, which represents passion and vitality. This phase is commonly associated with puberty, a time of intense emotions and self-discovery. It marks the awakening of passion and the beginning of experimenting and testing one's beliefs and abilities in the world. The energy of this stage is dynamic and vibrant, as individuals explore their desires and pursue their dreams.

4. THE WOUNDING

The fourth face of the soul, known as "the wounding," is a phase characterized by the extinguishing of the inner fire and the experience of pain and vulnerability. It is a time when the illusions of invincibility are shattered, often through significant life events. This phase cuts the umbilical cord that connects us to old beliefs and identities, leaving the soul wounded and bleeding. For some, this period may coincide with major life transitions, such as menopause or midlife crises, but it can occur at any age. The wounds inflicted during this phase may last a lifetime if left unhealed, impacting one's emotional and spiritual well-being indefinitely.

5. THE SHADOW

The fifth face of the soul, known as "the shadow," represents a phase where the inner wounds and unresolved issues come to the surface, demanding to be healed. It is a period of descent into the depths of our being, confronting dark and lifeless places within ourselves. To heal, we must acknowledge and embrace our shadow, listen to the wisdom of our soul and understand why these wounds occurred.

Without spiritual awareness, many remain trapped in denial, unable to heal. Only by delving deeply within and reconnecting with our true essence can we heal, transcend, and transform, allowing our authentic selves to emerge and guide our path forward in the world.

6. THE DOUBLE

The sixth face of the soul, known as "the double," is like a mirror with two faces. It reflects our journey of emerging from the shadow of the past into a moment of fullness. After experiencing and exploring life and making the necessary mistakes, we arrive at a place where we can fully embrace our true selves and embody wisdom.

7. THE REMAIN

The final face of the soul, known as "the remain," appears at the time of our passing. If we choose not to depart, the soul simply waits. At the end of life, it is this face of the soul that guides us out of the body. While often referred to as death, "the remain" navigates our journey of growth, collects our unique patterns, and chooses our next incarnation.

Moving beyond the faces of the soul signifies transcending and connecting with the divine. Beyond these faces lies the one face, which holds the secrets, resonance, and essence of being, encompassing destiny and true power.

JOURNEYING THROUGH FAIRY TALES FOR PERSONAL GROWTH

Fairy tales have been a profound source of inspiration for me since childhood. Visions of magical realms, where my imagination thrives, guide me on journeys of self-discovery and growth. These timeless tales spark my creativity, inviting me to explore the depths of my soul and uncover hidden truths. I embark on adventures through enchanted forests and on noble quests surrounded by mythical creatures. I am inspired to embrace my unique gifts and my own heroic odyssey. Fairy tales serve as mirrors reflecting the essence of my being, revealing pathways to transformation and enlightenment.

Listening to these compelling tales, I find solace, wisdom, and the courage to forge my destiny amid life's ever-unfolding mysteries. Fairy tales offer gifts by bridging the gap between the ordinary and the extraordinary, by weaving together threads of ancient myths with modern interpretations. Through their heros and monsters, these timeless stories speak to the deepest longings and fears of the human heart, illuminating the journey of separation and reunion with the divine. Each character embodies a facet of humanity, from the noblest virtues to the darkest vices, offering insights into the complexities of human nature. Fairy tales express our own struggles, triumphs, and aspirations, inviting us to explore the depths of our souls and discover the magic within ourselves.

I am the warrior, hero, princess, and more. I am an entire cast of fantastic characters such as dragons, elves, unicorns, giants, and witches. These stories, untethered from religious dogmas, serve as a beacon of love's triumph over fear. They weave an enchanting world where love reigns supreme, offering a glimpse into the most magical power humanity can ever know. The *Snow White* and *Sleeping Beauty* fairy tales portray the themes of beauty, innocence, love, and the triumph of good over evil.

In *Snow White*, we see the envy of the wicked queen, the kindness of the dwarfs, and Snow White's eventual awakening by true love's kiss. The story's themes are vanity, jealousy, and the power of love overcoming adversity.

Similarly, *Sleeping Beauty* portrays the story of a princess cursed by an evil fairy to sleep for 100 years until awakened by true love's kiss. It is a tale of waiting, enduring, and the eventual victory of love over the forces of darkness.

Both tales captivate us with their enchanting narratives and timeless lessons about courage, resilience, and the transformative power of love. In the context of the journey back to oneself, the seven dwarfs from *Snow White* stand for different aspects of the self.

1. **DOC** represents leadership and wisdom on the journey. He leads Snow White and the other dwafs, offering practical advice and direction. He symbolizes the rational mind or inner wisdom, which provides clarity and guidance.

2. **SNEEZY** represents delicacy and sensitivity. He reminds us that vulnerability is not a weakness, but can be a source of authenticity and self-connection.

3. **BASHFUL** embodies shyness. He struggles to express himself openly but finds courage through companionship and support. He symbolizes aspects of ourselves that are hesitant or fearful of revealing the true self, but can find strength through connection and self-acceptance.

4. **HAPPY** represents joy and positivity. His cheerful disposition uplifts the spirits

of those around him. In the inner journey, Happy represents the ability to find joy and contentment within oneself, even in the face of challenges.

5. **DOPEY** symbolizes innocence and purity of heart. He is childlike and playful, embodying simplicity and unconditional love. In the inner journey, Dopey represents the innate goodness within us that may have been overshadowed by life's experiences but can be rediscovered through self-love and acceptance.

6. **GRUMPY** reflects skepticism and resistance to change. He calls to mind the inner voice of doubt and fear that must be overcome.

7. **SLEEPY** represents rest and introspection. Sleepy reminds us of the need to pause and recharge on our path toward self-awareness.

Together, the seven dwarfs accompany Snow White on her journey of self-discovery, each offering valuable insights that parallel the challenges and revelations encountered on the path back to oneself.

The deepest healing and alignment of the self comes from a love that is intrinsic to our essence and inherent in our existence.

In many fairy tales, this transformative love embodies both masculine and feminine qualities: the prince symbolizes passion, while the princess represents wisdom and awareness. The love of the princess is not merely romantic, it is a recognition of the divine within and of the ability to see beyond external appearances to the true essence of the soul hidden beneath its earthly disguise.

When describing the journey toward self-realization, it is essential to convey the nonlinear nature of the process, emphasizing its gradual unfolding and transformative impact. As I travel through life, weaving my tales, I face various hurdles, societal norms, and beliefs that shape my perceptions. Yet, amid these external influences, there is also an inner compass guiding me—my soul's voice—urging me toward authenticity and growth, nudging me to transcend the limitations of personal and collective stories. The voice guides me in search of a deeper understanding of myself and my purpose.

The process of growing up and coming of age represents significant life stages, central to the narrative of fairy tales.

The Little Mermaid, for example, delves deeply into the complexity of human emotions and the challenges faced in fulfilling our heart's desires. Following the mermaid's journey, we witness her struggle with identity, sacrifice, and the pursuit of love. The story explores the theme of longing and the universal quest for fulfillment. In the most poignant moment of *The Little Mermaid*, Ariel sacrifices her voice and tail for the chance at love. This illustrates the weight of her choice and the consequences she is willing to face. The tale vividly portrays the struggle of balancing her desire to belong in the human world while still remaining true to herself. Through Ariel's journey, the story reflects on the importance of authenticity, the complexity of identity, and the quest for happiness and fulfillment amid life's challenges. It teaches lessons of self-discovery, courage, and the power of love.

The essence of *Rapunzel* lies in themes of isolation, longing, and liberation. Locked away in a tower by a witch, who symbolizes fear, Rapunzel still dreams about freedom and inner connection. Rapunzel's encounter with the prince is the catalyst for her liberation. His love for her motivates Rapunzel to take action and break free from the confines of her tower. This aspect of the tale underscores the transformative power of love and the courage it inspires in individuals to overcome oppression and pursue freedom and fulfillment.

In his book *The Masks of God*, Joseph Campbell emphasizes that the central theme of mythology is not solely focused on the challenges and trials of the hero's journey, but rather on the moments of realization and enlightenment that occur throughout the quest. Campbell suggests that mythology celebrates not just the struggles and deaths encountered by the hero, but also the moments of rebirth and resurrection that lead to greater understanding.

In the words of the Indian mystic Osho, *"Maturity means gaining your lost innocence again, reclaiming your paradise, and becoming a child again."*
According to Osho, *"Maturity has nothing to do with your life experiences. It has something to do with your inward journey, your experience of the inner. The more a man goes deeper into himself, the more mature he is."*

A JOURNEY TO LIBERATION

REVEALING LITTLE CLAUDIA'S WEB

In the depth of my meditation, a vivid tableau unfolds before me: I see a dense enigmatic forest, draped in shadows, where my little Claudia becomes ensnared in the intricate web of a cunning spider.

In her struggle to break free, she grapples with the sticky grasp of the web. Confusion clouds her mind, her body feels heavy and lifeless, and her heart beats with icy fear.

As she fights against the web's suffocating grip, little Claudia starts to release bright red droplets into a lake. Each one is a purification of the inner turmoil swirling in the depths of her consciousness.

I see a flame inside my heart giving me a glimpse of hope and trust, assuring me that I will someday win.
Everlasting, dwelling in my core, is a golden seed covered by the darkness of the night.
As I breathe deeply in and out, focused on dissolving the sticky threads of the web—my story, my thoughts, my feelings, and my experiences.
I feel my strength returning.
With each breath, I pull myself out of the web, reclaiming my freedom and self-empowerment.

Now I see myself walking through an open green field. Beautiful

trees dance along with the wind. I see blooming flowers celebrating, rejoicing in the return of spring.
I see birds flying in the sky, landing in the grass for a quick rest.
Deer are hiding themselves behind the trees; squirrels are climbing up and down.

I feel so free!
My deepest desire is to embrace it all!

~

In another scene, I see a figure standing at the end of a long line, a beggar draped in dust. In this tableau the man, though last in line, emerges as the first to ask for help, symbolizing a readiness to support others in his lineage. This marks a pivotal moment, beginning the healing of an era of disconnection and fear.

In this weary state, burdened by a heavy sack, the beggar approaches me with an air of exhaustion. As he draws closer, the contents of his load remain concealed. Despite this, I invite him to engage in conversation. With gentle concern, I address the stranger, sensing his bewilderment and troubles.

"What weighs on your mind, dear stranger?" I inquire softly.
"And what secrets does your bag hold?"
Surprisingly, his demeanor shifts, as he finds solace in the simple acknowledgment of his existence and inner turmoil.
As I look more closely, beyond his outward despair, I discern a radiant infant in his bag, glowing with innocence.
In a tender moment, he entrusts the child to me, imploring me to love, nurture, and care for him, revealing his own inability to do so.

This vision depicts the beggar as someone without wealth and as a symbol of my ancestor's struggles, spiritual disconnection, and deep emptiness in life. In this moment, I understand that the beggar carries more than his own troubles. He symbolizes parts of a legacy I am meant to mend and rekindle—a journey toward healing and rediscovering life's true meaning.

> **In a simple moment of stillness amid the chaos, Little Claudia starts her journey out of the menacing labyrinth. With each inhale and exhale, she gathers courage, drawing from her inner reservoir of strength. Gradually, she begins to wiggle her fingers, then her toes, reclaiming control over her body.**
>
> **Next, she focuses on her thoughts, untangling the webs of confusion one by one as she relaxes and lets go, liberating herself, regaining clarity and determination. As her heart gradually opens, she finds solace in the warmth of self-compassion and the gentle embrace of inner peace. With each step forward, she unravels the threads of fear that once bound her, emerging into the light with newfound resilience and a sense of self-empowerment.**
>
> **In this transformative moment, I envision a flock of seagulls encircling Little Claudia, symbolizing a divine affirmation of her journey. As they soar above, forming a circle of protection and guidance, I feel a surge of clarity and purpose.**

I recognize the vertical path ahead, a North Star guiding my ascension to higher levels of consciousness, propelled by my newfound understanding. With each step, I embrace the longing to nurture my heart, soul, and spirit, anchoring myself to a profound yearning to reconnect with my source, the sacred place that I instinctively call home.

In meditation, I see Little Claudia stepping into a dwelling divided between light and shadow. Here, she journeys through contrasting emotions and experiences, navigating moments of clarity and confusion, hope and despair, illumination and obscurity.
The house symbolizes the complexity of her inner world and the choices she encounters on her path of self-discovery and growth.
In one half, illumination brings comfort, while the darkness of the other half breeds a palpable fear of the unseen, swirling through her thoughts like shadowy bats. Her heart feels frozen.
Amid these experiences, she encounters the spectral figure of Mother Mary. Despite her stark pallor and rigid body, Mary's message resonates clearly: "LOVE YOURSELF!"

This message leaves Little Claudia with a new longing, as her heart now sees the possibility of her dream coming true.
Her journey feels like a carriage speeding down a perilous path, going through mud and obstacles that hinder progress and cause turmoil along the way.
Despite the weariness, her steadfast decision to reconnect remains unwavering. The message about self-love puzzles her, leaving her intrigued and reflective.
She turns inward, searching for the answer, and a gentle voice whispers, "Love is the essence of your being."
She inquires…"Is it that simple?"
Mary now replies with a soft smile, her eyes twinkling, and with true wisdom, she whispers, "Yes, dear one, it is that simple.
Love is your essence, your birthright, and your true nature."
Mary's words echo softly, "To uncover the depths of your being, you must shed the layers of conditioning and expectation that cloak your essence. Embrace vulnerability, for it is in the rawness of your truth that you will find the greatest liberation."

How can I make sense of this riddle, embracing vulnerability and authenticity?
How can I shy away from the swell, exploring the depths of my soul?
How can I unweave the web?
How can I stop the loom?
How can I calm the rolling of the waves of the ocean within?

> **Descending into the underworld of Little Claudia's dreams and imagination, I encounter monsters taking shape, their misty figures invading her thoughts and senses with colors, vibrations, and textures.**

I accept the openness of Little Claudia's vulnerability, exploring the depths of her soul, and untangling the complexities of her mind and emotions. I release anything that no longer serves her growth and well-being. I decide to practice mindfulness and being present. In this moment, a feeling of an overwhelming love overtakes me.

Trusting the Gold: Uncovering Your Natural Goodness by Tara Brach is an enlightening book about spirituality. In the introduction she describes basic goodness as the essence of our being and the importance of embracing the inherent beauty within. She mentions a story about a clay Buddha statue in Bangkok. In the 1950s, the statue began to crack from the excessive heat and drought. When monks peered into the cracks, they were astonished to find a gleam of gold under the gray cloud of dust covering the statue's exterior.

The gleam of gold represents our true, divine blueprint, which has been covered for countless life cycles with layers of stories and impressions, like the plaster and clay put on the statue to protect it from invading armies. The knowledge of the statue's true meaning had been forgotten, yet the magic remained in the depths of the dormant original Buddha, and it came back to reveal its spirit. The gold Buddha was always there, waiting to be uncovered and rediscovered.

When we lose connection with our spirit, we naturally start to identify with our surroundings and the defenses we created, and we forget the innocent, tender, and creative heart we are trying to protect.

I see now how removing the dust of Little Claudia's impressions and expectations allows me to uncover and access the light and love of my true nature hidden deep within.

THE FORBIDDEN FRUIT

A TALE OF TEMPTATION AND TRANSFORMATION

In a secluded garden, nestled within the ebb and flow of time, stands an ancient apple tree. Its branches reach for the heavens like the arms of a forgotten deity.

Among its branches, the apple hangs—a symbol echoing ages past, signifying wisdom, affection, eternal essence, and the allure of temptation. This tree, shrouded in mystery and legend, bore fruit of such glamour that even the most steadfast souls were drawn to its forbidden bounty.

It grants knowledge beyond mortal comprehension; it unlocks the secret of the universe with but a single bite … a burden of wisdom too heavy for mortal shoulders to bear.

In ancient tales and religious texts apples never cease to puzzle with their different meanings and interpretations. Very often the apple appears as a mystical or forbidden fruit. The biblical connotation of an apple relays the consequences of disobeying God's guidance. The punishment of exile from Paradise, mortality, and sin followed the tasty bites of the apple that Adam and Eve could not resist.

In ancient Greek mythology, on the other hand, the apple appears as an optimistic symbol of love, as well as an emblem of ecstasy, fertility, and abundance. It is the favorite fruit of the Greek god Dionysus, who offered apples to win the goddess Aphrodite's love and attention. To the ancient Greeks, an apple exemplified the passion for living a life that is inconceivable without love. This love that is not necessarily romantic or sexual, but rather a passionate love of the self and love of life.

As author Neale Donald Walsch advises: *"Never deny passion, for that is to deny who you are, and who you truly want to be ... There is no reason to live if we do not express ourselves. Life becomes self-creative. Passion is the love that is spirit, it turns being into action."*

As I settle into my sacred space and close my eyes to meditate,
I am surrounded by the deep silence of a dense forest.
In this serene environment, I am cradled within the soothing indigo glow of a crystal cave. Amid the darkness, a flicker of light captures my attention, signaling the beginning of a profound spiritual journey. It feels as though a gentle energy is stirring within me, ready to be unlocked.
In the depths of the cave, I seek out the blueprint of my soul—the master plan of my life that holds the keys to my purpose, as well as lessons and healing. As I melt into my core, I find the gift of love.

"God loves birds and creates trees for them to land on. Men love birds and build cages to confine them."

The blueprint of my soul guides me in how to release the birds and treasure the gifts of freedom. My highest truth becomes my highest vision. Embracing change invokes transformation. I have come to realize that resistance only leads to stagnation. Nature is not concerned with success stories; instead, it embodies dynamic growth, with consciousness flowing through us for eternity.

I undergo change without clinging to anyone or anything. Having no attachment does not signify a lack of love, instead, it is an exceptional expression of true love. Living consciously allows me to break free from most subconscious habits and patterns.

My higher mind is my true North Star, which illuminates my path and points me toward the road to fulfillment. North symbolizes guidance, while south represents manifestation. Following the guidance of my North Star means getting closer to my full potential, for ultimate goodness in this lifetime, always in alignment with my true nature.

The unique gifts and qualities that I bring into this lifetime define my true nature and show me how to walk in this world, following my bliss, with a heart full of fire.

Love. Light. Joy.

I become aware of my soul's purpose and my heart's deepest desires, which I genuinely choose to experience in this lifetime. My challenges remind me that there are still fragments to be healed: all this and so much more for me to discover.

PART IV
INTEGRATING CONSCIOUSNESS AND PHYSIOLOGY

THE SCIENCE OF LIFE AND HEALING

Many thousands of years ago, in the tranquil embrace of the Himalayas, Vedic sages devoted years to meditation to explore the mysteries of inner life, to alleviate human suffering, and to illuminate the path toward a life of purpose and meaning.

In their sacred quest, they embarked upon a journey into the mystical realms of consciousness, where their inner being became a powerful laboratory. They orchestrated a delicate dance of purification and stabilization of their nervous system, awakening the fire of transformation.

In their journey of self-discovery, the Vedic sages cultivated their inner selves to unlock the full potential of human consciousness. Delving into the depths of awareness, they discovered that the human mind possesses the ability to settle into a state of perfect stillness, a realm beyond all perceptions, thoughts, and feelings, while maintaining complete alertness and wakefulness.

In the vast expanse of pure consciousness, likened to a flat ocean, we encounter a profound sense of tranquility and serenity. In this state the mind is undisturbed by ripples of thoughts and emotions. The mind stretches into infinity, embracing the boundless depths of awareness and the limitless possibilities that exist within. True and transformative healing happens on that level.

As the mystic poet William Blake articulated, *"If the doors of perception were cleansed, everything would appear to man as it is, Infinite."*

In the gentle teachings of Maharishi Mahesh Yogi, wisdom unfolds like petals revealing the essence of life: perception is the mirror of our consciousness. Thoughts emerge, traverse the corridors of our mind, and intertwine with our emotions, shaping our perception of reality.

As we ascend to higher levels of vibration, we immerse ourselves in a realm where happiness, joy, and love become our constant companions. Here we encounter bliss and self-realization, healing and transformation. As we heal our scars, we find ourselves firmly anchored in a state of contentment.

At the innermost core of the mind resides the essence of nature itself, a field of unity from which springs the infinite diversity of the universe. Mountains, oceans, flowers, stars—all emerge from this primordial field, weaving a tapestry of interconnectedness and beauty.

AYURVEDA

Over time, the Vedic sages began to impart the wisdom of healing through Ayurveda, the "science of life." Often hailed as the mother of healing, Ayurveda embraces a holistic approach to well-being that focuses on achieving balance and harmony within the body, mind, and spirit to promote overall health.

Ayurveda, originating from ancient India, is a holistic system of medicine. Its essence lies in the belief that each person is unique, and therefore their health and wellness needs are also unique. Ayurveda seeks to maintain or restore balance through various practices including diet, herbal remedies, lifestyle modifications, yoga, meditation, and many different types of massage.

The core principles of Ayurveda revolve around the three doshas—vata, pitta, and kapha—which represent different combinations of the elements of space, air, fire, water, and earth and their influence on bodily functions. By understanding our dosha constitution and making adjustments to align with nature's rhythms, we can use Ayurveda to prevent disease and promote vitality, longevity, and spiritual growth.

VATA is associated with qualities like dryness, coldness, lightness, and vitality. Vata imbalances can lead to anxiety, insomnia, and digestive issues.

PITTA is characterized by qualities such as heat, intensity, sharpness, and oiliness. Balanced pitta fosters intelligence, courage, and decisiveness. Excessive pitta can result in anger, inflammation, and heartburn.

KAPHA embodies qualities of heaviness, slowness, stability, and moisture. In balance, kapha promotes calmness, strength, and nurturing. Imbalances may manifest as lethargy, weight gain, and respiratory issues.

MY EXPERIENCE WITH AYURVEDA

Since 1995 I have been regularly going to The Raj, a Maharishi Ayurveda health center in Fairfield, Iowa, for panchakarma. Panchakarma is a deeply rejuvenating program in Ayurveda, tailored to cleanse the body of accumulated toxins and restore balance to the doshas. These fundamental energies govern physiological and psychological functions. Panchakarma typically involves a series of treatments including massage, herbal therapy, dietary adjustments, and cleansing techniques administered over a period of several days or weeks. The procedures aim to eliminate impurities from the body, strengthen the immune system, and promote overall health and well-being.

My personal experience with Ayurveda has been truly transformative and enriching. Its knowledge has provided me with a concrete spiritual and mental foundation, guiding me to understand the intricate laws and rhythms of nature. Through Ayurveda, I have found support on my path to enlightenment. The knowledge of daily and seasonal routines provides me with a deep sense of connection to the cosmic order.

The detoxification practices I have experienced through Ayurveda have transformed me, cleansing my body, clearing my mind, and soothing my emotions. The process brings my physiology closer to its innate intelligence, leading to healing and a newfound lightness of being. During periods of cleansing, I value the opportunity to focus on self-care, diving inward to nurture my spiritual, physical, and mental well-being.

MEDITATING, TRANSCENDING, UNITING

In the engaging tale of my life, meditation emerges as a cherished companion, bestowing upon me countless blessings and enriching the tapestry of my inner world. Through its gentle embrace, I forge a deep intimacy with myself. Happiness, bliss, and gratitude fill my heart with love and contentment, brightening my path toward self-reconnection and inner peace. Each moment spent in meditation nurtures and uplifts me, guiding me along this wondrous journey of self-uncovering.

About 50 years ago, when I first embarked on my meditation journey, it was a concept largely misunderstood by those around me. Many viewed meditation as a means of escaping reality and failed to recognize its significance for our overall well-being—spiritually, physically, and emotionally.

Yet, within the depths of my practice, I discovered a sanctuary of peace and clarity, where the noise of the world fades away and the tranquility of the present moment embraces me with open arms.

Meditation is not about stopping thoughts or trying to empty the mind entirely, but rather about observing thoughts as they arise without judgment. With regular practice, meditation can help reduce stress, improve concentration, enhance emotional well-being, and promote a greater sense of self and others.

Among the many meditation techniques I explored, each offered a unique journey into the depths of consciousness. I was fortunate to learn Transcendental Meditation® (TM), a technique pioneered by one of my earliest spiritual mentors, the revered Maharishi Mahesh Yogi. His teachings deeply resonated with me, laying a solid foundation for my spiritual growth. Through his wisdom and loving guidance, my mind expanded and my heart found healing and support, paving the way for a journey of life-altering transformation and self-reconnection.

TM stood out as a gentle and natural approach. It fosters inner peace and clarity, inviting practitioners to dive into the depths of their conciousness with ease and grace. I am forever grateful for the presence and teachings of Maharishi Mahesh Yogi in my life!

In the wisdom shared by Maharishi Mahesh Yogi, spiritual awakening and

unfoldment extend beyond mere growth. They encompass the expansion of the mind and the opening of the heart to higher states of consciousness. TM leads us toward a deeper understanding of our true nature and the boundless potential within. The seven states of consciousness brought to light by Maharishi Mahesh Yogi are:

1. WAKING CONSCIOUSNESS

In the waking state, we engage with the external world through our senses, perceiving its vibrancy and diversity. Amid life's offerings and boundless opportunities for joy, excitement ebbs and flows, reminding us of the transient nature of all experiences. All is temporary.

2. DREAMING CONSCIOUSNESS

A state of consciousness characterized by the mind creating and experiencing various dream scenarios and events.

3. DEEP SLEEP CONSCIOUSNESS

The state of deep sleep, in which there is no conscious awareness of the external world or internal thoughts. The deep sleep state of consciousness is essential for our survival. It is meant to rejuvenate our body, release stress, and revitalize the mind in order for us to meet our everyday challenges.

4. TRANSCENDENTAL CONSCIOUSNESS

The fourth state of consciousness, beyond waking, dreaming, and deep sleep, is characterized by pure consciousness, inner peace, and transcendence of thought. It is a state of restful awareness. This state of transcendental consciousness, as described by Maharishi Mahesh Yogi, is a state of pure awareness, where the individual mind transcends all mental activity and experiences a state of deep unbounded awareness. The body settles into a state of deep rest, while the mind remains fully alert and awake. It is a state of perfect inner silence, bliss, and harmony. Over time these qualities can be integrated into our daily lives.

5. COSMIC CONSCIOUSNESS

In cosmic consciousness our individual consciousness merges with the universal consciousness, experiencing inner peace and expanded awareness all the time. This state brings a sense of freedom and bliss. It is a transformative experience that reshapes our perception of ourselves, evoking feelings of gratitude and worthiness, happiness, and love.

6. GOD CONSCIOUSNESS

In the state of god consciousness, we transcend our individual identity and directly perceive and merge with the divine. This involves refining our senses to perceive subtle levels of reality, where we encounter radiant beings and experience the presence of light. As we draw closer to the source, our sense of bliss deepens, and even the simplest experiences become imbued with joy. We feel gratitude and appreciation for all aspects of life, and our hearts overflow with devotion. This state brings us closer to the ultimate realization of unity consciousness.

7. UNITY CONSCIOUSNESS

Unity consciousness represents the pinnacle of consciousness, where one realizes the ultimate truth of oneness with all existence, transcending individuality and duality. In this state we perceive the interconnectedness of all creation, recognizing that we are inseparable from the universe. It is described as the highest level of relative reality, characterized by infinite and absolute vibrancy. Unity consciousness is a state of continuous awakening, growth, evolution, expansion, and deepening, where the realization of oneness continually unfolds and enriches our experience of existence.

In *The Supreme Awakening*, Craig Pearson highlights an experience of unity consciousness described by a practitioner of TM: *"Objects seem transparent, and I perceive unboundedness, the unmanifest, in everything I see.... Nothing seems foreign to me; I feel at home with everything, everyone, and with any situation."* This experience suggests a deep sense of interconnectedness and unity with the entire universe.

One of the passages perhaps most worth recalling about the impact of the unity of consciousness was written by Ralph Waldo Emerson. In his 1841 essay "The

Over-Soul," the transcendentalist poet and philosopher proclaimed that, *"Within man is the soul of the whole; the wise silence; the universal beauty to which every part and particle is equally related; the eternal One. And this deep power in which we exist, and whose beatitude is all accessible to us, is not only self-sufficing and perfect in every hour, but the act of seeing and the thing seen, the seer and the spectacle, the subject and the object, are one. We see the world piece by piece, as the sun, the moon, the animal, the tree; but the whole, of which these are the shining parts, is the soul."*

As we ascend the spiral pathways of consciousness, it becomes clear that on each level we find a progressive stage of awakening and enlightenment. Each one leads to a distinctive new world of experiences and knowledge and each corresponds to a unique physiology.

It is fascinating how deepening my meditation practice can alter my perception in such a positive way, enhancing my connection to the world and the people around me. This shift in perception, seeing the world shine more brightly and feeling a stronger affection for humanity, highlights the impact that mindfulness and meditation can have on my outlook and emotional well-being.

Eckhart Tolle's teachings emphasize the importance of letting go and surrendering to the present moment. He encourages us to recognize that the past is merely a story we tell ourselves, and the future exists only as thoughts in our minds.

The true essence of life lies in the present moment—the *Now*—where we should direct our focus entirely. When our attention is consumed by the past or future, we risk losing touch with the reality of now, which holds the potential for the deepest happiness and fulfillment. By embracing the present moment fully, we can access a profound sense of peace and contentment that transcends time and circumstance.

PART V
FINDING RESOLUTION

CELEBRATING MY REUNIFIED SELF

> **I wander along a tranquil pathway, framed by majestic pine trees. I approach a house designed with grand glass windows and pristine white marble floors.**
>
> **From the outside, its interior appears vacant. Upon opening the door, I meet my masculine counterpart, who has been patiently awaiting my arrival. A sense of belonging fills our hearts as we dance—the merging of loving hearts and passionate spirits igniting a mystical union. In the flames of our fervent dance, a new depth of love is discovered, leaving my heart replete and whole.**
>
> **The agony of past divisions dissolves into a joyous explosion of unity and jubilation. This awakening becomes the culmination of my pursuit for love, and my inner happiness wells up from the depths of my being—a wellspring of inspiration and liberation. I feel free.**

My vision beautifully illustrates the transformative power of the integration of masculine and feminine energies into a harmonious balance that brings out the best qualities of each of them. It highlights how different energies can complement and enhance each other. This unification of the nurturing and passionate attributes of myself result in a single, balanced expression that supports my personal growth. The sacred dance of the masculine and feminine are within me, the merging of both leads me back to unity.

Love, the highest vibration, is an expression of evolution itself.

My visions spring from a deep well of self-love. They shed light on my path, guiding my choices, and unlocking doors to inner freedom. They ignite my longing to heal, grow, and embrace life fully. With each step, as I raise my vibration, I feel a primal joy that transcends ego. It surges from my heart, infusing my entire being with vibrant energy and boundless happiness.

We create our future by embracing a higher vibration of consciousness, which will bring new information, new insights, and new opportunities.

Passion is the love that turns being into action.
Passion changes concepts into experience.
Passion is the fire that drives us to express who we are!

Evolution is about aligning ourselves with our future.... It is already there!
My higher self shows me solutions with simplicity, depth, unconditional love, support, and encouragement.
The words come freely, with no judgment.

Enlightenment does not come from the mind, the ego.
It comes from the heart.
Love... Self-love...
Self-love is about aligning with source energy...
Embracing and connecting with who I truly am.
It is pure love... marked by the absence of resistance and the presence of wholehearted acceptance.

To create a work of art I must love it.
My gifts show who I am and how I define myself.
There is only a single magic, the healing power of love,
Love's divine alchemy.
Do not shy from its radiant glow, nor flee from its embrace.
Surrender to it!
Suffering melts away in love's tender hug,
as we awaken to our essence, our truest grace.

ACKNOWLEDGMENTS

In this journey of words and wisdom, my heart overflows with gratitude to the countless souls, extraordinary teachers, mentors, and guides who have dedicated themselves to their own inner healing, naturally elevating the consciousness of humanity through their inner light and connection to truth. Their wisdom has been a guiding light on my path.

I extent my heartfelt thanks to Michael, who lovingly assisted me in structuring this book, weaving together my 30 notebooks filled with writings, insights, and visions—a difficult task that he performed with grace and patience.

Thanks to Nicole, whose radiating presence and bright intellect has truly helped put this book together.

A special thanks to my dear and loving sons, who enrich my journey with their boundless gifts and unconditional love. Each step is brighter because of their presence. I am appreciative of Humberto, my ex-husband for teaching me the essence of self-love. I am deeply grateful for the unwavering support of my loving parents and the nurturing care of my friends.

To Wendy, my dear friend who introduced me to Suzy and Frederico, my diligent editor and the creative director at Pointed Leaf Press. Thank you for helping me sculpt my original vision for this book into a final, polished form. Your insights and expertise have been invaluable.

Finally, my deepest gratitude goes to the universe for its astounding support, for bringing incredible people and opportunities into my life, and making this journey possible and profoundly enriching. —**Claudia Faria Carvalho**, September 2024

ABOUT THE AUTHOR

Claudia Faria Carvalho was born and raised in the vibrant landscapes of Brazil, a land filled with natural wonders and the dense foliage of the Amazon. A yearning for greater freedom to explore and express herself pulled her away from the familiar comforts of Brazil, setting her on a transformative journey to New York, where she has lived for the past 40 years, continuously expanding her horizons and deepening her intimacy with the world around her.

Carvalho's quest for self-reconnection has been diverse, involving various techniques aimed at restructuring personal consciousness. She attended continuing education classes in psychology at the C. G. Jung Institute of New York. She has delved into past-life regression, embraced meditation, studied yoga philosophy and metaphysics, and attended workshops and lectures that significantly deepened her connection to the spiritual dimensions of life.

In addition, a transformative three-year program in Ayurveda and Vedic science at the Maharishi Institute of Vedic Science in Boston, Massachusetts, further expanded her insights and enhanced her well-being.

BIBLIOGRAPHY AND RECOMMENDED READING

Brach, Tara. *Trusting the Gold: Uncovering Your Natural Goodness.* Boulder, CO: Sounds True, 2021.

Cavafy, Constantine P. trans. Edmund Keeley. "Ithaka." Original in *Gramatta*, Alexandria, Egypt, 1911.

Emerson, Ralph Waldo. "The Over-Soul." From *Essays: First Series*, 1841.

Homer. trans. Emily Wilson. *The Odyssey.* New York: W. W. Norton, 2018.

Lao Tzu. trans. Jonathan Star. *Tao Te Ching: The Definitive Edition.* New York: Jeremy P. Tarcher/Penguin, 2001.

Osho. *Maturity: The Responsibility of Being Oneself.* Insights for a New Way of Living. New York: St. Martin's Griffin, 1999.

Pearson, Craig. *The Supreme Awakening: Experiences of Enlightenment throughout Time—And How You Can Cultivate Them.* Fairfield, IA: Maharishi University of Management Press, 2013.

Roads, Michael J. *Pan ... and Me: Metaphysical Adventures with the Spirit of Nature.* Portland, OR: Six Degrees Publishing Group, 2023.

Walsch, Neale Donald. *The Complete Conversations with God: An Uncommon Dialogue.* New York: Penguin Group, 2005.

These books provide a variety of perspectives on spirituality and personal growth, offering insights that can profoundly transform perception and enhance quality of life.

JOSEPH CAMPBELL
- *Transformations of Myth through Time*
- *The Hero with a Thousand Faces*
- *The Power of Myth*

DEEPAK CHOPRA
- *Quantum Healing: Exploring the Frontiers of Mind/Body Medicine*
- *Synchrodestiny: Harnessing the Infinite Power of Coincidence to Create Miracles*

PAULO COELHO
- *The Alchemist*

RAM DASS
- *Be Here Now*

JOE DISPENZA
- *The Habit of Being Yourself: How to Lose Your Mind and Create a New One*
- *Becoming Supernatural: How Common People Are Doing the Uncommon*

THICH NHAT HANH
- *The Art of Living*
- *Reconcilitation: Healing the Inner Child*

CARL G. JUNG
- *Memories, Dreams, Reflections*
- *The Archetypes and the Collective Unconscious The Secret of the Golden Flower (A Chinese Book of Life)*, trans. Richard Wilhelm

MAHARISHI MAHESH YOGI
- *Science of Being and Art of Living: Transcendental Meditation*
- *Maharishi Mahesh Yogi on the Bhagavad-Gita: A New Translation and Commentary, Chapters 1–6*
- *Love and God*

SWAMI MUKTANANDA
- *Play of Consciousness: A Spiritual Autobiography*
- *Where Are You Going?: A Guide to the Spiritual Journey*
- *I Am That: The Science of Hamsa from the Vijnana Bhairava*

OSHO
- *Meditation: The First and Last Freedom*
- *Tantra: The Supreme Understanding*
- *Love, Freedom, Aloneness: The Koan of Relationships*

M. SCOTT PECK, MD
- *The Road Less Traveled*

MICHAEL J. ROADS
- *Through the Eyes of Love: Journeying with Pan*

MICHAEL SINGER
- *The Untethered Soul: The Journey Beyond Yourself*
- *Living Untethered: Beyond the Human Predicament*
- *The Surrender Experiment: My Journey into Life's Perfection*

ECKHART TOLLE
- *The Power of Now: A Guide to Spiritual Enlightenment*
- *A New Earth: Awakening to Your Life's Purpose*

MARIANNE WILLIAMSON
- *A Return to Love: Reflections on the Principles of "A Course in Miracles"*

PARAMAHANSA YOGANANDA
- *Autobiography of a Yogi*

INDEX

Adam, 82, 135
Amazon, Brazil, 23
Ananda, 32
Aphrodite, 135
Athena, 72, 73
Ayurveda, 48, 142, 143
  kapha, 142, 143
  panchakarma, 143
  pitta, 142
  vata, 142

Baba, Neem Karoli, 103
Bali, Indonesia, 52
Bangkok, Thailand, 51, 132
banyan tree, 51
Blake, William, 141
Brach, Tara, 132
  Trusting the Gold: Uncovering Your Natural Goodness, 132
Buddha, 73, 132
Buddhism, *see* Buddhist practices, 51, 52
  karma, 51, 55

C. G. Jung Institute of New York, 36
Campbell, Joseph, 76, 122, 126
  The Masks of God, 122
Cavafy, Constantine P., 65
  "Ithaka," 65
Cervantes, 103
chi, 72
Chidvilasananda, Gurumayi, 41
Chopra, Deepak, 41, 72
Cyclops, 51

Dalai Lama, 108
Dionysus, 135

Eastern philosophy, *see* Eastern traditions, 52, 55
Einstein, Albert, 107, 111
Emerson, Ralph Waldo, 81, 148
  "The Over-Soul," 149
Eve, 82, 135

Gaia, 51
Garden of Eden, *see* Paradise, 82, 135
Ganges River, India, 42
Ghats, 42
God, 24, 88, 104, 107, 135, 136
Greek mythology, 51, 135

Himalaya Mountains, 141
Hinduism, 52
  Balinese Hinduism, 52
Homer, 72
  The Odyssey, 72

Ithaca, Greece, 73

Jesus, 69, 70, 73
Jung, Carl, 82

King Arthur, 72, 73
King Jr., Martin Luther, 81

Lazaris, 111, 112
  "The Seven Faces of the Soul," 111, 112
Lao-Tzu, 95, 99
  Tao Te Ching, 95
Little Mermaid, The, 122

Maharishi Mahesh Yogi, 41, 48, 76, 100, 108, 141, 143, 144, 147
meditation, *see* meditate, 13, 41, 48, 52, 55, 67, 69, 87, 96, 100, 103, 104, 108, 126, 131, 137, 141, 142, 143, 144, 149
Merlin, 72, 73
Mother Mary, 131
Muhammad, 73

New York, 36, 69, 70

Osho, 126

Pearson, Craig, 148
  The Supreme Awakening, 148
Proust, Marcel, 58

The Raj, Fairfield, Iowa, 143
Rapunzel, 122
Roads, Michael, 27
  Pan … and Me, 27

Shiva, 42
Sleeping Beauty, 118
Snow White, 118, 121
Star, Jonathan, 96

Titans, 51
Tolle, Eckhart, 41, 149
Transcendental Meditation, *see* TM, 48, 100, 144, 147, 148
  cosmic consciousness, 147
  deep sleep consciousness, 147
  dreaming consciousness, 147
  god consciousness, 148
  transcendental consciousness, 147
  unity consciousness, 148
  waking consciousness, 147

Varanasi, India, 42
Vedic philosophy, *see* Vedic tradition, 45, 48, 141, 142
  atman, 45, 48
  brahman, 45, 48
  dharma, 23, 45
  karma, 45, 55
  moksha, 45

Walsch, Neale Donald, 136
Western philosophy, *see* Western tradition, 52, 55
Wilde, Oscar, 58
Wizard of Oz, The, 73

yoga, 48, 142
Yogananda, Paramahansa, 41

PUBLISHER Suzanne Slesin
CREATIVE DIRECTOR Frederico Farina
EDITORIAL ASSISTANT Julian Cosma
COPY EDITOR Amelia Kutschbach

ISBN 978-1-938461-64-4
LIBRARY OF CONGRESS NUMBER 2024917861
First Edition
Printed in Spain

An Open Heart: The Key to Self-Love © 2024 Claudia Faria Carvalho. All rights reserved under international copyrights conventions. No part of this book, or any of its contents, may be reproduced, utilized, or transmitted in any form or by any means, electronic or mechanical, including photocopying, recording, or by any information storage and retrieval system, or otherwise, without permission in writing from the publisher. Please direct inquiries to info@pointedleafpress.com.
Pointed Leaf Press, LLC. 136 Baxter Street, Suite 1C, New York, New York 10013.